Watch the companion film trailer, *Breaking the Silence*
www.myamishstory.com

My AMISH Story

Register This New Book

Benefits of Registering*

- ✓ FREE accidental **loss replacement**
- ✓ FREE **audiobook** – *Pilgrim's Progress,* audiobook edition
- ✓ FREE information about new titles and other **freebies**

www.anekopress.com/new-book-registration

*See our website for requirements and limitations.

My
AMISH
Story

Breaking Generations of Silence

Rebecca Borntrager Graber

ANEKO
PRESS

We love hearing from our readers. Please contact us
at www.anekopress.com/questions-comments with
any questions, comments, or suggestions.

Contents

Acknowledgements

And they overcame him by the blood of the Lamb and by the word of their testimony. Revelation 12:11

First and foremost, I praise and thank God for His grace that made it possible for there to be a story worth telling and for the inspiration to keep putting words on paper when the memories proved difficult.

My gratitude goes to my husband for the hours of typing and retyping he did to prepare the manuscript for the publishers. It looked like an insurmountable task to me, but you made it look easy.

I thank Joseph for making it all happen: finding a publisher, being my sounding board, and even writing parts of the book.

Ruth, thank you for allowing me to glean from your journals and for your suggestions and help with proofreading.

To Dorcas go heartfelt thanks for pushing me out of the bakery and trading my kneading bowl for a computer.

And finally to the publisher and editors of Aneko Press, thank you for walking me through the steps to get a book written and published.

I dedicate this book to my Dad, David S. Borntrager. He taught me how to read the Bible, pray, and diligently seek after God's truth.

Foreword

Five hundred years ago, Martin Luther tacked a piece of paper on the door of the church in Wittenberg, Germany. The ideas listed on that piece of paper changed the world in general and my world in particular.

One idea especially impacted my family – the idea that the Scriptures should be available to everyone in a language they understand. Centuries ago, when my ancestors in Switzerland began to read the Bible in their common language and tried to live according to what they read, the church reacted and expelled them from their communities and churches. Eventually, the Amish church emerged from these turbulent times.

Down through the centuries, the Amish church slowly changed. When I (Joseph, the oldest son of Lester and Rebecca) was a boy, I spoke a dialect of German called Pennsylvania Dutch until I was seven years old. Then I learned English in order to start school. When I was in third grade, my mother taught me my third language, German, so I would be able to read Martin Luther's German Bible. Like many other Amish people, I learned German well enough to pronounce the words, but I really struggled with understanding what I was reading, because we never actually spoke German. We only used it to read the Bible and a few other church-related documents.

As I grew older, I noticed that my dad began to read the Bible in English. Of my three languages, English was the only one we used for speaking, reading, and writing, so it made sense that he wanted to read in a language he understood better than the archaic German. Over the course of several years, Dad's life changed – for the better. But when he preached the things he read in the Bible in the Amish church, turbulent times ensued for us, and in 1994 my parents were excommunicated by the Amish church.

My father, Lester Graber, didn't tack a piece of paper on any church door – the Amish don't have church buildings, so there was no door – but in a very real sense, he followed in the footsteps of Luther. This book tells my father's story – the story of an Amish preacher and the woman who stood by his side as he embraced the reformation in the twentieth century.

Joseph Graber, son of Lester and Rebecca Graber

Author's Note

In case you were involved in the events of this book and think "That's not the way it happened," let me simply say this: I wrote it as I remember it. Some names and identifying details have been changed to protect the privacy of individuals.

Introduction

The majestic moose lifted his head at the sound of voices. The rattle of lunch boxes and bike wheels on the gravel alerted the creature from the forest, as he quenched his thirst at the lake's edge. Water dripped from his hairy lips, as he surveyed the clearing across the lake. The sight of the schoolchildren emerging from behind the trees caused the huge animal to shake his massive rack of antlers and retreat to the shadows of the tall pine trees that covered the mountainside.

The quietness of the afternoon was shattered when three of the youngsters broke from the group and came pedaling down the incline between the twin lakes where the crystal-clear waters reflected fluffy white clouds in the blue, blue western sky. The bikers continued up the next hill, past the lakes, and up the driveway where they dropped their bikes by the gate, which led to a little, one-story cabin nestled at the foot of the mountain.

Minutes after the children entered the house, the door opened again and a lone figure emerged. The look of determination and purpose on her face matched her resolute strides as she headed up the trail leading to the top of the mountain.

She strode along, oblivious to the chattering squirrels that leapt from tree to tree. A lone Gray Jay screeched, as he left his perch at her approach and flew away over the tall treetops. Halfway up the mountain her steps faltered. A shudder passed through her body as she leaned against the rough bark of a tall pine tree at the edge of the trail. She bowed her head, a groan escaped her lips, and her shoulders heaved.

After a moment, she shook herself, straightened her shoulders, and with an effort continued her way up the trail. Her steps were slower as she picked her way over a fallen tree and the surrounding debris and trudged up the mountainside. She kept brushing her hand across her forehead, as if to get rid of plaguing thoughts.

She paused at the edge of a small clearing and scrutinized the forest floor carpeted with pine needles, before she walked over to a fallen log that rested in a bed of ferns. She sank down and held her head in her hands. After a long moment the silence was broken, as she lifted her head, raised her eyes to heaven, and whispered, "Help me, Lord."

She dropped her head into her hands again and took a deep breath. Then with a sudden resolution, she got to her feet, threw her head back, and stretched her hands towards the heavens. She cried out, "Oh God! Heavenly Father! I can't do it! It's too much. Why does it have to be this way? Please, Lord, just take us all home to be with You. Now!"

CHAPTER 1

The Last Amish Family

On a blustery Sunday afternoon in the boot heel of Missouri, Lester Graber and two of his children walked across the field back to their house where his wife Rebecca and the rest of the children awaited him. Lester was an Amish minister, and the last Amish man left in the community.

A little less than a year before, this settlement showed potential to grow as more Amish people moved into the community. Initially, jobs on a chicken farm in the area were the drawing card. Owners of the chicken farm furnished houses plus wages, which provided a good way for struggling young families to get ahead financially. When problems arose between the manager and employees, family after family left for other places. Once Rebecca's dad moved out, it seemed to seal the fate of this little Amish community.

Lester opened the door and walked into the house; a gust of wind stirred the living room curtains. Rebecca looked up from putting food on the table. Their eyes met, but they said nothing. No words were needed. They'd already said everything several times.

After the other Old Order Amish families moved out, a group

of Beachy Amish families had moved in. Lester and Rebecca went to one of their church services, and Lester wanted to join them. Their church services were in English, and the members seemed to understand the Bible and love each other. After that first visit, Lester thought, "Why not now?" But Rebecca harbored concerns.

"Sure, they have Bible studies, support missionaries, and evangelize more than the Amish do, but they still have fences. They're just set a little farther out than the ones we have," Rebecca reasoned. "Those man-made rules and traditions that don't make biblical sense are still there."

After that first Sunday, she didn't go back, but Lester took some of the children a few more times. He was drawn to them and the way they opened the Bible and discussed it in all their meetings.

When they first moved to Missouri, Lester had decided to really study the Bible and write an Amish Ordinance Letter that was completely biblical and completely Amish. Early in the mornings and late at night, he worked on it. But the more he read the Bible, the more frustrated he became. Why did the Amish do things the way they did?

CHAPTER 2

The Call to Montana

One Monday afternoon, Rebecca walked to the mailbox to mail her weekly letter to her dad. Her thoughts wandered. Despite all their previous conversations, Lester and Rebecca had worked on the *Ordnungs Brief* (church standard letter) again the night before. After hours of rehashing, they still hadn't found the Scripture needed to support all the traditions, which kept the Amish church as it had to be to stay Amish.

Rebecca opened the mailbox. To her surprise, the mailman had already come and gone. She pulled out a handwritten letter postmarked from Montana and went to find her husband. When Lester caught a glimpse of his wife waving a letter at him, he stopped the sawmill. He accepted the letter with some curiosity and sat on a log to open it. His calloused fingers tore open the envelope and unfolded the handwritten letter. Rebecca looked over his shoulder, and together they read the words that would change the course of their lives.

The Amish church in Montana needed a preacher. If Lester came to fill that role, they would provide him with housing and a job.

The rest of the day as Rebecca went about her work, her

thoughts centered on the letter from Montana. *It all seems so unreal.* She once met a family who had lived on the West Kootenai in Montana when the community first started. They'd written a book that she read. The idea of living in Montana sounded like an adventure that only happened to people in books. *But now this letter. Can it be a possibility? Is this direction from God – an answer to our prayers?*

Then another letter arrived. This one from the schoolteacher in Montana. He explained how the church had been without a minister for quite some time and they really needed spiritual oversight. If Lester came, it would be an answer to their prayers on the West Kootenai.

As they talked it over, Rebecca felt this was a way to honor her father and stay Amish, while perhaps being more biblical. Both letters from Montana seemed to be written by Christians who knew the Scriptures.

Lester thought it seemed like a great opportunity and a new start. Maybe the church in Montana would follow the Bible more closely.

As for the children, the news excited Joseph. He began dreaming of all the new birds that he would be able to add to his birding list. Besides this, the church in Montana allowed their members to have bicycles. Joseph imagined himself with a group of boys speeding along a mountain trail on their bikes.

Though Rachel always welcomed an adventure, Ruth wasn't so thrilled with the thought of moving again. She hated change. It had been hard to leave Tennessee to come to Missouri. Now the thought of going to some far-off place with the weird name of Kootenai didn't appeal to her at all.

They all contemplated the move in their own way, but in the days ahead, they'd all have to work together to prepare for the auction to sell some of their belongings in order to make the trek west.

CHAPTER 3

Westward Bound

White lines stretched along the road in front of them. The engine of the black van strained to pull the trailer loaded with everything the Graber family needed to start a new life in Montana. As an Amish preacher, Lester wasn't driving. His friend Joe was a member of the Beachy Amish Church who were allowed to have cars. They used the family van to move, and Joe drove while Lester sat in the front passenger seat.

They entered Wyoming from South Dakota and confronted the foothills of the Black Hills. The van struggled with its load and started to overheat.

Joe's brow knit into worry lines. "This van hasn't done this before."

"You're pulling a bigger load than usual." Lester let out a sigh.

"Well, yes. But I didn't think it would get hot this quick."

By the time they reached Billings, Montana, the problem grew severe enough that Joe looked for a U-Haul dealer. He pulled in, parked the van, and rented a truck to continue the trip.

Once on their way, Lester stared at the rugged landscape. "It's a good thing you got the truck. Look how big these mountains are getting."

"They're bigger than I imagined," Joe admitted.

As they drove into town with mountains in the background, the buildings seemed smaller than those back East. It was their first experience seeing the Rocky Mountains, and everything took on a new perspective. Doors appeared lower and the buildings looked smaller. When they stopped at a gas station, they asked the man, "Are these buildings regular size, or are they built on a smaller scale?" The man assured them that they were built on the same scale as buildings across the United States.

"They sure look small, what with the mountains in the background," Lester said.

"Yes." Joe shook his head in disbelief. "I was almost sure they were smaller, but I guess that guy knows what he is talking about."

Joe stroked his beard as he took it all in. "If these hills are this big, compared to the buildings, no wonder my van overheated."

"No doubt." Lester nodded.

Even the Water Is Different

The miles wore on, and Lester's thoughts drifted to the past – to his first move. It was 1965, and he was seven years old. His family moved from Middlebury, Indiana, to Clark, Missouri. The moon seemed so bright that night on the train. Although his mother told him it was the same moon they saw in Indiana, he wasn't sure he could believe her.

Lester spent all of his school days in Missouri. That's where his mother was buried, after she died of cancer in 1969.

Middlebury, Indiana. Clark, Missouri. Bronson, Michigan. Then back to Indiana, this time in LaGrange County. These were the places he lived as he grew up. Four Amish communities. Four different levels of conservatism and rules. How did it all fit?

After getting married, he and his family lived in other Amish communities. Tennessee. Arkansas. Texas. Michigan. Then

Tennessee again. All with different rules. All convinced they were right. Questions from his boyhood nagged him. *Maybe I'll find answers in Montana.* He was glad to be moving again, excited by the possibilities.

As they traveled on, miles of water came into view; the sign said it was Flathead Lake. "Look at that water," Lester said. "What makes it so bluish green?"

"Maybe it's not muddy like we're used to seeing back in Missouri," Joe said.

By the time they came through Kalispell and Whitefish, they grew more accustomed to the mountains, but as they traveled north toward the Tobacco Valley around Eureka, one sight after another still amazed them. Rising as a backdrop from the valley floor, the Whitefish Range on the right reached to the sky. Very tall, especially to these Midwesterners who were used to large flat fields of corn that stretched for miles. A hill in Puxico, Missouri, was a slight rise in the road compared to these mountains.

West Kootenai Valley

Rebecca sang softly under her breath; she sang the words of a well-known hymn. She sang about the woods and forests; she sang about the birds and trees; she even sang about the streams and mountains. Rebecca worshiped God, her Savior, and praised Him for His greatness.

She changed a word here and there to fit her mood at the moment, as she watched the mountains come nearer and nearer.

When they pulled into the parking lot of a convenience store, she watched Joe and Lester walk inside and marveled that the doorway was tall enough for her husband to enter without stooping. Her senses struggled to adjust to her surreal surroundings; she was awed at the grandeur of the mountains and the beauty of the West. Even more so, she was overwhelmed by the step they were taking. Rebecca felt like a pioneer, venturing into the unknown, leaving behind family and all things known and familiar. They didn't know anybody in Montana. The letters they had exchanged with the men on the Kootenai were the only tangible connection they had with anyone in this part of the country.

She didn't know of any Amish settlement farther west than Kansas. *This settlement, being so far removed from the other Amish settlements . . . maybe, just maybe, they will be different. Hopefully they will be more spiritual, living here in the mountains and closer to God.*

The men walked back to the truck and said they had another thirty-mile drive to get to their destination. *Thirty more miles, then I'll have to meet strangers and be friendly.* She loved traveling, in spite of carsickness, but she dreaded meeting people. Her husband had the knack of never meeting a stranger, and she was thankful for that. He always knew what to say and made friends quickly.

Although that could have its drawbacks too, she thought to herself as they pulled back onto the road. She thought about his friendliness with the Beachy Amish. One of the reasons she had so readily agreed to come west was that it felt safer to get away from those Beachy Amish people with whom Lester had become so friendly.

Yes, many things in the Amish church troubled her – many things she wished were different. But the things that bothered her most in the Amish church were in the Beachy church too, just on a different level. Rebecca was glad she could honor her father by staying with the old ways. Besides, she loved the Amish lifestyle with its horses and buggies. It was just some of the unscriptural practices that bothered her.

CHAPTER 4

Songs of Hope

Rebecca nervously tucked a stray strand of hair behind her ear and checked to make sure Rachel's cap strings were tied. She glanced at Ruth, knowing she shared her feelings of intimidation when she met strangers. It didn't help that they were dressed in clothes very obviously made according to different church rules than the people living here.

They had attended services with their new church for the first time that morning. Rebecca would have gladly relaxed at home that evening, but Lester was eager to get to know the people better, and ministers were expected to attend the Sunday night singings.

She paused and looked past the tall pine trees at the mountains silhouetted against the evening sky. She'd much rather go on a hike to explore unfamiliar trails than walk into a houseful of strangers. She took a deep breath and followed her husband.

They entered the room, and Rebecca checked to see on which side the women sat. To her surprise, the men and women sat together. Back East the women always sat on one side of the room and the men on the other. She liked this. Now she wouldn't have to worry about what to say to strangers. Lester would be at her side to do the talking, if anybody wanted to visit with them.

Someone passed them a songbook, and the singing began. They had been to a lot of singings in a lot of places, but this surpassed them all. Rebecca wanted to simply sit back and listen, as the strong young voices rose and fell in perfect harmony. She forgot all about the differences in their clothes and that she was a stranger in a strange land. It felt as if her very soul was being lifted on the swells of the songs and carried away, far above the mountains.

Joseph enthusiastically found the pages and sang along. It encouraged Rebecca, as she envisioned her oldest son, along with his sisters, learning to sing as well as these young people. She glanced at Ruth, who to her delight, had also forgotten her shyness, as she eyed some cute little babies she longed to get in her arms. Oh, how Ruth loved babies.

Rebecca smiled to herself and thought about how happy Ruth would be with their little one soon to be added to the family. Then she could cuddle to her heart's content. Rachel squirmed beside her mother and eyed the little girls in anticipation of making new friends as quickly as possible; little Jonathan stayed content as long as he was close to his Mama.

"There is a God! He is alive!
In Him we live; and we survive."

The deep bass of the young men rolled through the house before being joined by the sweet harmony of the young ladies. Lester knew singing four-part harmony pushed the line a lot further than had been allowed in any of the previous communities they had lived in. *But it's true. There is a God, and He is alive. Maybe here we can truly live according to Scripture.* He joined his voice in the melody.

As they left the singing later that night, Lester hummed beneath his breath. Maybe they could be Amish and biblical at the same time after all.

CHAPTER 5

I Just Wanted to See the Bear

One Saturday morning Joseph bounded into the house after feeding the chickens. "Let's hurry and get our chores done!" Ruth looked up from cleaning the stove and drilled him with a hard stare. "As if you're the one to tell us to hurry." Joseph often frustrated Ruth, because of how long he took to get his chores done, but Joseph's excitement wasn't dampened by her remark.

"We can still see the tracks Kauffman's wagon made when they went on their picnic yesterday." Joseph gathered the plates from the breakfast table. "We could follow them and go see Arnold's Pond. That's where Michael said they were going."

"It's your turn to wash dishes," Rachel said as she quickly cleared the table. "I want to go too. May I go with you?"

Joseph carried the plates to the sink. "If Mom says so, but I really don't know how far it is." He reached for the dishwashing detergent. The dishes clattered and the dust flew as Ruth, Joseph, and Rachel hurried through their Saturday chores.

By early afternoon, the house sparkled, and they were free to go. They quietly hurried from the house where their little brother, Jonathan, was napping on the couch. Ruth, Joseph, and Rachel walked past the garden and followed the tracks the

Kauffman's team of horses and box wagon made the day before. The old national forest access road wound across Young Creek and up the mountain.

As the trail dipped into the dark forest, the three fell silent. They instinctively felt they were entering the domain of wild things. This was Montana after all. There could be bears and mountain lions out here. Joseph felt a little uncertain about what to do if they actually saw a wild animal. Part of him wanted to see a bear or some other wild animal, but at the same time, he wondered if it would be safe if it actually happened.

"What if we see a bear?" Rachel broke the silence. The other two looked at her, then at each other. Joseph decided that, as the older brother, he couldn't afford to appear afraid.

"Well, if we see a bear, we'll write it on our list of animals we've seen. That would be exciting." He hoped his voice sounded bolder than he felt.

Just then a raven flew overhead, and their eyes followed it across the creek. This was the first place they'd lived that had ravens, and you could hear its wings fanning the air.

"The wagon tracks cross the creek." Ruth pointed across the creek. "Are we going over there?"

The others looked to see where Ruth pointed, and the three of them decided to brave it.

When their bare feet touched the water, it was very cold. "Must be snow melting from the mountains to make this water so cold." Ruth read a lot so the others were used to her sharing interesting trivia about things.

After they crossed the creek, Joseph had an idea. He looked around until he found a dark stump in the distant woods. Trying to sound surprised, he pointed and yelped, "Hey! Look over there." The other two quickly peered into the shadows where he pointed. Ruth looked skeptically at Joseph. He laughed a little, "Don't you see the bear?"

"There's no bear." Rachel kept walking.

As they marched along, they tried to scare each other by pretending to see bears and mountain lions. They also pointed out different birds, trees, and plants that were new to them.

Walking to the outside and a little in front, Ruth stopped suddenly when they came to a bend in the road. "There's a bear!" she said breathlessly.

"Yeah, right!" Joseph wasn't about to get tricked by his sister. But there was something about the way she stood and the tone of her voice that almost convinced him. He stepped beside her and followed her wide-eyed stare.

"It is a bear!" he said.

About a hundred yards ahead a black bear stood watching them. For a long moment, they stood like statues, staring at the brown nose of the bear, pointed in their direction. Joseph and Ruth looked at each other, not sure what to do.

Then they turned to look at Rachel. She wasn't there! They spotted her back down the trail just in time to see her disappear around a bend. With one final glance at the bear and each other, they turned and ran.

***

Peace and quiet settled over the house as Rebecca sat at the quilt. It was a good feeling to have the floors mopped, the windows sparkling, and everything clean and in its place. Outside two Gray Jays squawked in a fir tree, and somewhere in the back yard, a squirrel chattered.

Inside, the only sounds were Jonathan's deep rhythmic breathing, as he slept, curled up on the corner of the couch, the ticking of the clock, and her thread being pulled through the quilt.

A sigh of contentment escaped Rebecca's lips, as she adjusted her chair and threaded her needle. *This is so peaceful and restful,* she thought to herself. She hardly finished the thought, when feet pounded on the front walks. Rachel burst through the door and collapsed on the couch near her sleeping brother and gasped, "There's a bear."

Ruth and Joseph ran in right behind Rachel. "We saw a bear," Joseph exclaimed excitedly.

"At first I thought it was a cow," Ruth added breathlessly.

"Did the bear follow you?" Rebecca asked. "Was there more than one?"

Ruth and Joseph looked at each other. "We just saw one, and I don't think it followed us." Ruth began.

Joseph finished between breaths. "We ran so fast – trying to catch up with Rachel – we didn't really see which way it went."

A sob and a sniffle from the couch drew Rebecca's attention to Rachel who had buried her face in the couch cushions with her shoulders heaving.

She walked over and sat beside Rachel. "Don't worry." She rested a reassuring hand on her shoulder. "I don't think the bear will come here. He was probably just as scared of you as you were of him."

"I-I-I'm not sc-sc-scared." Rachel sobbed as she buried her face deeper in the cushion.

"Well, what's wrong then? Did you hurt yourself? Why are you crying?"

"I j-j-just wanted, I just w-w-wanted to see the bear!" Rachel sat up as she choked back her sobs. "When they said there's a bear, I ran so fast I didn't even see the bear."

"You didn't see the bear?" Rebecca asked and tried to hide the smile tugging at her lips.

"No, I didn't, and I want to." Rachel sat up and dried her eyes. "Can we go back and see if it's still there?" she asked eagerly.

Rebecca glanced out at the long shadows cast by the tall pines with the sun slipping behind the mountain.

"Maybe another day," she told her young daughter. "It's too close to dark now."

CHAPTER 6

My Sheep Hear My Voice

L ester rested the New Testament he was reading on his chest, closed his eyes, and leaned back in the recliner. He pondered the words from the tenth chapter of the gospel of John.

If anybody tried to enter the sheepfold in any way other than through the door, which was Jesus, he was a thief and a robber. Lester's mind followed the logic of that truth. *So, if we try to make our own way by our traditions and man-made rules, does that mean we are thieves and robbers? How can I tell people how to hear His voice? Am I a good shepherd? I don't want to be a hireling, but being the newest arrival here, how much authority do I really have?*

The words of Jesus seemed to hold so much promise. Yet there was division among the Jews because of what He said. *That sounds familiar.*

The more Lester got to know the people in this community, the more he heard a difference of opinion. As a shepherd of the flock, he had to guard against divisions. He knew there were disagreements, and he wanted to bring the people together.

When Rebecca settled at the quilt, he roused himself from his musing and pulled up a chair. She smiled as she picked up her needle. He said, "What do you think about this Sunday school situation?"

Rebecca thoughtfully checked her thread. "We've never lived in a community that had Sunday school before." She looked Lester in the eyes. "We were always taught that it leads to modernism and liberalism. Why do they want it?"

"Well, that's just it. They started it when they didn't have a preacher for church services, and they still wanted to get together. Then some of them liked it so much they wanted to continue." Lester paused to remember. "The men who are for it say that a few others won't have anything to do with it, but I haven't really heard anyone's reasoning."

"I can almost hear my brother say that young people who aren't ordained by God could get big-headed, if they're allowed to discuss the Bible in front of everybody. They'll get to thinking they are smarter than the older men." For a moment, voices from the past swirled around in Rebecca's memory. "But, reading the Bible and discussing it is a good thing!" she declared emphatically.

Lester ran his fingers through his hair. "The other day Ora Jay told me they started Sunday school here before we came, because there was no minister living here. During the winter months, there would be no visiting ministers from back East like in the summertime. They wanted to have church somehow, so they read the prescribed Scriptures and let each of the married men take part in the discussion. But now we have a minister, and they want to continue the in-between Sundays, while some of the families don't want to have any part in it."

Rebecca rethreaded her needle. "Wouldn't it be better for the community to get together to study the Bible than go after worldly amusements on a Sunday? Especially if so many of the people who've been here a long time seem to desire it."

Lester rubbed the back of his neck. "I should probably go directly to each of the older members and ask their opinion on the matter in order to unite the whole community." Lester stood up, glad to have found a point of action. Maybe this is what Jesus meant when He said ministers were to be shepherds.

"Yes, then we can see if there's a possibility of coming to an agreement." Rebecca agreed with a nod.

Sunday School

Throughout the week, Lester watched for opportunities to discuss the Sunday school issue with each of the men. Some of the younger men were surprised that the minister would actually ask their opinion and then listen to what they had to say. Maybe the new minister would be a good thing for the community.

By Saturday evening, Lester fostered a new excitement. As Rebecca gave him his haircut, he talked about what he'd learned. "The men who weren't participating feel strongly that the Sunday school shouldn't be led by a layman, but an ordained preacher should lead it, and I am an ordained preacher."

He paused a moment, as Rebecca trimmed around his ears. "As long as I lead the service, all the other men can still share what they think about the Scripture." Lester's voice rose in jubilation. "And they have all agreed to come under those conditions."

That Sunday Lester announced that Sunday school services would be held the next Sunday. With a few adjustments in the order of the services, the whole community could participate in unity.

Sure enough, the following Sunday those who usually resisted the idea of Sunday school arrived with everybody else. They enjoyed an encouraging time, reading and discussing the Scriptures.

Later that night, a prayer of thanksgiving ascended toward heaven from the Graber house. "Thank you, Lord, for letting Your sheep hear Your voice."

CHAPTER 7

It's Getting Colder

Joseph clambered down the ladder from the loft where he slept. "Mom, look at this." He struggled to slip his arms into his coat, which he'd dug out of the box of winter clothes. "See." He stretched out his arms to show his mother the sleeves were about two inches too short.

Rebecca glanced out the window at the ground, white with frost. It wasn't officially winter yet, but it sure felt like it. The days grew colder and coats were needed, especially in the mornings.

"I guess you'll have to wear my everyday coat while I make you a new one," she said. "I'm so glad I sent that order off to Stauffer's the other day. It should be here any day now; then I'll have everything I need to make new school coats for all of you."

"We'll need bikes, too," Joseph said. "Everybody rides bikes to school here."

"You would think we would always have plenty of bikes, since we own the bike shop," Rebecca commented thoughtfully.

"You might think that," Ruth said. "But actually, it works the other way. Dad rents out our bikes, when he runs out of rentals."

"Like the shoemaker's children going barefoot," Rebecca mused.

When the Graber family moved into the place vacated by the Kauffmans, they took over the local bike shop where visitors rented bikes for a week or all summer. Lester also kept bike parts on hand and repaired bikes for people.

"I asked Dad which bike will be mine," Rachel's voice was muffled as she rummaged through a box of boots, looking for her pair. "He said a bunch of bikes are coming back, because the summer tourists are leaving, so we'll have plenty of bikes."

"Hard telling what shape the bikes will be in when they're returned," Joseph said as he tried on his mother's coat. "Some people are just plain hard on bikes."

"That's because they aren't used to riding bikes," Rebecca said as she straightened Joseph's coat collar and checked the length of the sleeves. "But I haven't seen a bike yet that your dad couldn't fix."

"At least there's one bike that should be in good shape when it comes back," Lester said as he walked in just in time to hear the last part of the conversation.

"Why? What bike?" Rebecca eyed her husband.

Lester chuckled. "Well, there's this preacher from back East who likes to come out here every summer. They don't allow bikes in his church at home, and he says he doesn't even ride the bike. But he likes to see a bike setting on his porch, knowing that he has one if he ever wanted to try riding it."

"He pays rent just to have a bike to look at?" Rebecca asked with eyes wide.

"That's what he told me." Lester chuckled again. "Which is fine with me."

CHAPTER 8

Her Favorite Season

That afternoon Rebecca and Jonathan gathered pine cones and twigs from under the trees between the shop and house for kindling. Autumn in Montana was so different than autumn in Missouri or Tennessee. Here, as soon as the sun slipped behind the mountains, it grew so chilly that a fire felt good.

With both buckets full of kindling, Rebecca straightened her back and gazed at the tree-covered mountainside. The forests surrounding the West Kootenai Valley had many different kinds of trees, but most were evergreens. A minute later her husband and one of the bachelors stepped out of Lester's bike shop for a quick test ride on a bike he had repaired.

Rebecca turned her attention from the trees and asked, "How can there even be a noticeable difference in the trees as the seasons change?"

"Oh, don't worry," the bachelor said. "There'll be some color in these mountains a few weeks from now."

"What do you mean?" For a moment, Rebecca wasn't sure if he was serious.

"There's a tree around here called the Larch tree, and it

drops all of its needles every year. Turns yellow, just like all those trees back East. You'll see."

His words proved true. In the coming weeks, some of the trees near the house changed color. While the mountainsides didn't display the spectacular canopy of colors found in the Tennessee hills or the Ozarks, they had a breathtaking beauty of their own, and the splashes of yellow made it look more like fall.

Fall was her favorite season. She relished the excitement of getting ready for winter – getting everything in order and stocked up for the long winter ahead. It was a challenge she enjoyed. But this fall an uneasiness troubled her. They usually had hundreds of jars of fruits and vegetables, canned and lined up on the shelves. Plus, piles of squash, potatoes, onions, and cabbage were on hand. Their last two moves made it impossible to grow a garden, and it left them with a lot of empty jars. And this was Montana – the winters could get really cold and long. One of the bachelors said, "It sometimes drops to forty below."

As her mind raced to figure out how to utilize the available food, Rebecca thought, *I'll have to trust that the Lord will provide.*

Their stores included bags of rice, beans, wheat, and oats. *A person could live on rice and beans,* she figured. And the wheat would be ground for flour for bread and baking. Oatmeal made a good breakfast in granola or cooked for hot cereal. Oatmeal could also be used for baking. For greens, they could use alfalfa seeds to grow alfalfa sprouts, and they still had some canned green beans. Milk could be bought from the neighbors, which they could turn into butter, yogurt, and cheese. *And as long as the chickens keep laying, we'll have eggs.*

With the canned peaches and grape juice, desserts could be made using the bucket of tapioca pearls. Yes, they had more food than the Ingalls family did in *The Long Winter,* but it was still going to be a challenge, especially with lunches to pack for school and work.

Winter Approaches

As winter approached, it meant getting school clothes ready and making thick winter coats. Rebecca kept the sewing machine busy, but the older children were worried about their clothes being different from the other children's clothes. She tried to make bonnets for the girls more like the bonnets worn in this community and shirts for the boys with lay down collars; but as fall progressed, it was harder and harder to get everything done before the time of the baby's arrival. As usual, the baby was in no hurry to get there. According to her calculations, she was usually closer to ten months than nine months.

Maybe I'm half horse, she ruefully thought as she waddled laboriously from the sewing machine to the table where she had the materials spread out. She also needed to find those big curtains to close off one end of the living room for her parents, when they came. Her stepmom had been there to help at the birth of all their babies. A live-in midwife was something to be appreciated, but this time, Grandpa and Grandma Borntrager had to travel all the way from Tennessee to Montana to be there to welcome the new baby at the Graber house. Even though her dad liked to travel, and he usually headed south by this time, he loved his family enough that he agreed to bring Mom to Montana, so they wouldn't need to have a stranger for a midwife or go to the hospital. It was so far to the nearest hospital or doctor that it wouldn't be very feasible anyway.

Rebecca's excitement grew as she anticipated being able to spend time with her dad to discuss some things which weighed on her heart. It had been more than a year since she'd seen her parents.

CHAPTER 9

The Nature Hike

Joseph sat at his desk and gazed out at the finches on the bird feeder outside the schoolhouse window. Teacher John helped the lower graders finish their morning lessons. For once, Joseph had finished all his work quickly and taken advantage of his time to sketch a cliff scene on the back cover of his notebook.

He pulled out the little book where he kept his bird list. He had also started an animal list and hoped to make new entries in both lists today. Joseph glanced across at Michael who focused on finishing his lesson. In front of him, Eli checked his own bird list. Joseph knew Eli had six more birds than he did. *Eli has such sharp eyes. Maybe today I can catch up.* Today was nature hike day at Mountain View School, and they were all excited.

The students walked by pairs in a row along Whitetail Drive. Once they reached the woods, they walked heel-to-toe, moving through the woods as quietly as possible. Joseph walked next to his friend Michael. They had their little notebooks with them and scanned for sightings of any birds or animals they could add to their lists. The bird and animal lists were part of the nature assignment Teacher John had given them.

Joseph tried to use "splatter vision" to find any movement in the trees, when Michael jabbed him with his elbow. One of the rules of the nature hike was to limit talking, and the students all followed the lead of Teacher John. He motioned everyone to leave the trail. Joseph and Michael carefully stepped into the trees in the direction Teacher John motioned. Through the trees, Joseph spotted a small lake of very dirty water. Alkali Lake was a watering hole for a lot of wild life. If they were really quiet, perhaps they might just see some.

A commotion down the line by the older students drew Eli's attention. He pointed, and then Joseph saw it. A bear ambled out of the woods on the south side of the lake. Right behind her followed two cubs. Up and down the line, students poked their partners and pointed, but the excited whispers alerted the bear. She swung her head slowly around and sniffed the air. All the students held their breath, until she continued on her path down to the water.

Ruth froze in her tracks as she saw the bear and her cubs. She remembered how Rachel had missed seeing the other bear and turned her head slowly to make sure Rachel didn't miss seeing this one. Farther back in the line of students, Rachel wore a rapt expression as she stood on her toes to get a better view. Not only did her sister get to see a real live bear in the woods, but she saw a mama bear with twin cubs too.

Another message went down the line. Teacher John motioned again and formed a silent, "Follow me" with his lips.

Very carefully, the line of students walked along the trail on the west side of the lake. In a few moments, they reached a place that offered a better view of the lake. As they left the path, Joseph surveyed the lakeside for movement. He spotted some deer on the other side and there, right in front of him down by the water, stood the bear and her cubs. For the next several minutes, the students watched as the furry little cubs tussled with each other and then tumbled after their mother.

Once the bear left, Teacher John gathered the students around and lifted the silence. The students broke out in excited chatter with each other. "A bear!" "With two cubs!"

Joseph grabbed his pencil and wrote in his notebook: "Black Bear with two cubs – Alkali Lake."

Teacher John spoke loud enough for all the children to hear. "Today's assignment in the woods is to find a tiny tree you can uproot and plant in a pot back at school." It was time to find their trees.

As the students broke rank to find little trees, Ruth paused to admire some pretty pink flowers growing in the clearing by the lake. She had seen pictures in a bird book of flowers like these with a bright yellow goldfinch perched on them. She marveled at the beautiful color combination. If she planted one of these plants close to their house, it might attract a goldfinch. Her dream of seeing a real live goldfinch on a plant with pink flowers might be fulfilled. *What a lovely thought.*

But what would her mother say if she transplanted a thistle plant? It was a thistle plant, and thistles were weeds to be gotten rid of. Taking one last look at the flowers, she joined her schoolmates in the quest for a small tree.

Back at school, Michael carefully tucked in the last bit of soil around his little tree in the pot. He looked at Joseph, "I'm going to talk to my tree every day and breathe on it, so it will grow better!" They laughed, remembering the conversation the adults had the previous Sunday about trees needing carbon dioxide.

Joseph agreed, "I'm going to make mine grow so big I'll need a new pot!" The boys laughed together. Nature hike Fridays were the best, and Teacher John was a great teacher.

CHAPTER 10

Waiting for the Baby

D on't your fingers get cold when you ride your bike in this frosty weather?" Grandpa asked, as Rachel hurried for the door to go to school.

"Yes, but I can't find my gloves, and I don't want to be late," Rachel grabbed the doorknob to head out.

"Here, take mine," Grandma offered, as she walked into the living room with her own gloves. "Then we'll find yours for tomorrow."

Grandpa followed Rachel outdoors and helped her steady her bike, while she strapped her lunch box on the rack; then he watched her whiz off. A bit wobbly at first, but she gained her balance, and Ruth and Joseph followed behind.

It was good for the whole family to have Grandpa and Grandma to help them. Lester had to go to work so early he couldn't take the children to school or bring them home if it snowed or turned cold. And it was comforting for everyone to know Rebecca wouldn't be alone when the baby came.

Grandma always busied herself with writing or piecing the quilt she brought from Tennessee. She also had orders for the tatted, cross bookmarks that she crafted so beautifully. Yes, Grandma always found something to do, as did Grandpa.

Grandpa worked in the shop to put together a stronger quilt frame, which worked better for Rebecca. It was easier for one person to use than the old one; it was also longer, so she could make king and queen sized quilts. Rebecca's Great Uncle Clemens had fashioned the ends and the little sprocket wheels to fit onto the ends of the sticks, but the sticks were too long to transport on the bus, so Grandpa put the frame together after he arrived at their house. Grandpa also did a lot of reading and writing, while he stayed close to the fire because cold weather bothered his back.

Ice formed along the banks of the lakes and soon froze over. The children grew excited about ice-skating and coasting. Days stretched into weeks, and one morning they woke to find the ground covered with snow.

Grandpa worried they might get snowed in, and he longed for the warm sunshine of the South, which would ease the pain of his aching back that only grew worse when the weather turned cold. But he wasn't a complainer. Instead, he took advantage of the joys that could be had by whatever life dealt him. He dug an old sleigh out from behind the bike shop and fixed a few things on it. Then he hitched Root Beer, the pony, to it and tested it. It glided easily over the snow. He'd be able to take the children to school on the coldest days. One more thing Rebecca was grateful for. Now she didn't have to worry about the children getting so cold that they'd get sick and have to miss school. Ruth especially didn't want to miss any days because she had never been absent or tardy. Her cousin Truman never missed a day in all of his eight years, and Ruth wanted to do the same thing.

One morning after it snowed all night, the deep snow made it too difficult to use their bikes, so the children left their bikes at home and trudged through the snow to school. When Ruth,

Joseph, and Rachel were dismissed from school that afternoon, they bundled up and got ready for a cold trek home back through the snow. But when they stepped outside, how surprised and delighted they were! Grandpa waited for them in the schoolyard with Root Beer hitched to a sleigh.

"Where did you get this sleigh?"

"Whose is it?"

"Oh, this is fun!"

They peppered Grandpa with questions and exclamations so fast that he just smiled and whistled softly under his breath, while he made sure everybody was tucked in snugly. He tightened the reins, clicked his tongue, and the pony pulled forward. They glided through the fluffy white snow and into a winter wonderland.

Snow piled on every pine tree branch and along fences and on top of mailboxes. Ruth sighed in contentment, snuggled under the heavy buggy robes, and listened to the squeaky sliding sound of the snow crunching under the runners of the sleigh. She felt like she was in a Thomas Kinkade painting.

That evening, after supper and dishes were done, Ruth spread a jigsaw puzzle on the table; she knew Grandma shared her love of putting puzzles together. As soon as Grandma joined her, all the children gathered around the table to help, because they all wanted to be close to Grandma.

Grandma had such a sympathetic ear for listening to all their tales of life – whether joys or woes. She also had a remedy for each little ache and pain. And when it came to learning something new, she was the most patient teacher. From a new recipe to learning to tie your shoelaces, her way of explaining things didn't make you feel stupid for not knowing it already.

Later that week when the children were in school and Lester was at work, Rebecca and Grandma discussed different things people had tried to start labor, if the baby seemed slow to come.

Grandma mentioned castor oil. Grandpa's ears perked up from the chair where he'd been reading *The Budget* newspaper and keeping wood on the fire.

Castor oil, he thought. *Wonder if they have some at the store?*

Grandpa grabbed his coat and hat and said, "I think I'll take a little ride with the sleigh."

After he left, the house grew very quiet. Grandma nodded over the letter she was writing, and Jonathan napped on the couch with deep rhythmic breathing.

Rebecca felt a familiar sensation in her lower abdomen. After a while, she got up from the quilt and walked around a bit. "Mom," she said, "I really do believe it's time."

Grandma instantly became alert and bustled to the kitchen to stir up the fire in the kitchen range. "Well, I wish Dad was here," she worried, as she peered out the window towards the driveway. "Oh, here he comes," she said with relief as he marched through the snow on the path.

Grandpa came in, and after taking off his coat, he handed Rebecca a small paper bag. Mystified she opened it and looked inside. He watched her with a twinkle in his eye.

She pulled out a bottle of castor oil. "You don't have to take it, if you don't want to," he said.

She smiled. "Well, I think my contractions have already started."

"Oh my, that worked faster than I thought it would," he said and took the castor oil and put it back in the bag.

That afternoon while Ruth, Joseph, Rachel, and Jonathan had fun ice-skating with their friends and neighbors at the lake, a baby girl joined the Graber family. They named her Rosemary.

Once Rosemary arrived, Grandpa could finally take Grandma to the sunny South for the rest of the winter. Before he left, he had something on his heart that troubled him deeply, and he brought it up that last morning before they left.

He started out by cautioning about some of the more modern or worldly practices in the church. One thing could so easily lead to more. "And, I can't help but be troubled with all the bikes being used instead of horses," he said with tears choking his voice. "This time I see a row of bikes lined up in front of the house. Will I see a row of cars and trucks there the next time I come?" His voice broke with emotion.

His words stabbed Rebecca's heart, as if someone had thrown a dagger at her. *Does he really think we would leave the Amish? Is that all the faith he has in us?* His words so stunned Rebecca that she couldn't say a word in reply.

In the months to come, those words echoed over and over in her mind. Not so much the words themselves but the pain and anguish she heard in her dad's voice. It left her heart filled with a heavy foreboding as she bid her parents farewell. She didn't know it then, but that was the last time they would ever come for a real visit – a visit where they would sleep in their bed and eat at their table.

CHAPTER 11

The Bachelors of Bachelor Hill

The crunch of bike tires in the driveway and footsteps on the front porch brought Rebecca out of her reverie. She pulled the thread through the quilt, and her hand paused mid-air. The door opened, and a straw hat whizzed through the air and landed on the floor, halfway between the doorway and the quilt where she sat.

The perplexed look on her face turned to cheerful amusement, when a young man appeared in the doorway. With a grin on his face, he paused to say, "Well, I guess it's safe to come in, since my hat didn't come flying back out." Everybody enjoyed a good laugh, and they welcomed him in and invited him to stay for supper.

Lester and the young man kept a lively conversation going all evening, while Rebecca and the children listened and kept busy with the evening tasks of getting supper on the table and doing the dishes afterward.

How fascinating to hear all the stories about the bachelors on Bachelor Hill. Rebecca was especially eager to hear these stories. It would give her something more interesting to write to those back East than just the weather and where church was held on Sunday.

Lester worked with some of the young men on his job, but he also connected with these bachelors more and more, when they came to the bike shop to get parts and repairs. Because he frequently invited them to stay for a meal, the rest of the family became acquainted with them also.

Some of these young men came to the Kootenai Valley seeking adventure. The excitement of living in a cabin in the mountains and going hunting for big game lured many of them. Others came to get away from a bad situation at home and in the settlements where they grew up. Some had been jilted, and others were just tired of all the church factions.

Most of these bachelors were fine young men with good intentions, but because they came from such a variety of Amish settlements, some of the elders in church were driven to distraction by thinking they had to hold them accountable to all the rules of the churches they came from. This caused so much tension that many of the young men avoided church altogether whenever possible.

From two to three dozen of these bachelors lived in various accommodations, anything from a one-room cabin to a two-story, beautifully built, log house with a balcony. Some were brothers sharing a cabin while others were friends. Some preferred living by themselves.

Lester wasn't there to judge them. With his general interest in people, he never met a stranger and easily became friends with these bachelors. In return for their friendship, they kept the Graber family supplied with meat. Rebecca was grateful for that, since Lester wasn't a hunter. Usually the meat was very good, but once in a while Rebecca wondered if the gift of meat was just a way of getting rid of meat from an old deer that was tough or had a bitter taste because it hadn't been taken care of properly.

Then Lester got hurt one day at the sawmill and was laid off work for a while. Money became tight. Rebecca surveyed the pantry with concern. *How will I keep food on the table? God will have to provide.*

God Provides

Early one morning an unusual noise aroused Rebecca. She nudged Lester. "Did you hear that?" she asked sleepily.

"What?" Lester shot out of bed and stood on his feet so suddenly it startled her clear out of her sleep.

She perched on one elbow. "I heard a noise on the front porch. Listen." Together they listened in the darkness of the early morning and then stared at each other.

They clearly heard a deep, "Er, er-er- rooo!" from the front porch.

Their chickens were supposed to be in the henhouse behind the house. Had something gotten in and scattered them?

Lester found his flashlight and headed toward the door, and Rebecca's heart pounded with trepidation, as she followed him. He cautiously opened the front door. The buttery circle of light from the flashlight shined across a couple big boxes sitting on the porch. Beside them, something rustled inside a smaller box. As they hesitated, once more the deep throated, "Er, er-er- er- rooo!" sounded from the box. They looked at each other and laughed, as they carried the bigger boxes inside. The box with the rooster stayed outside. They opened the big boxes, and to their surprise, they were filled with groceries and food. Who had left the boxes on their porch?

Rebecca's heart overflowed with gratefulness, as she silently thanked God for providing for their needs.

CHAPTER 12

Cowboys and Ranchers

Joseph looked forward to the next summer with excitement. Every spring the ranchers in the West Kootenai Valley used horses to work their cows and move them to their summer leases on Forest Service Land. This year, Joseph would work with John Wayne Miller, one of the Amish ranchers who lived over in the Green Basin. Usually he rode his bicycle back and forth from the foot of the mountain down to the Green Basin, but for the cattle drive, he wanted to ride like a cowboy.

Lester had purchased a pony cart to use with their mountain pony, Root Beer. They used him for transportation, but since the whole family didn't fit on the cart, usually Ruth and Joseph rode their bikes when they all went somewhere.

The pony was trained to the saddle, but Joseph didn't have a saddle. He often rode bareback and sometimes used a pad, but for something as big and important as a cattle drive, he wanted a saddle.

It all started one Sunday afternoon when Rebecca heard the women talking about the cattle drive. As she had listened to the women and heard about how many wagons and buggies would be needed, how many people were going, and what they'd have to take to feed the men, she started thinking about it. *I'm sure Joseph would like to go. Actually, I'd like to go too, but I don't see how we could all go, so if I can somehow help Joseph make the connections he needs to be included, that'll be enough for us this year.* She wasn't surprised when Joseph mentioned it Monday morning and was prepared with a suggestion.

"Maybe you should talk with Dave Kauffman," Rebecca suggested. "Root Beer used to belong to Dave's grandson, so he might know where to find a saddle."

Joseph gathered up his courage and took the short cut through the woods to see Dave Kauffman. Dave listened to Joseph's request. "So, you need a saddle. Hmmm."

He started walking toward the old barn, but Joseph knew he kept the saddles in the new barn. However, Joseph decided not to say anything. Instead, he hid his disappointment, followed Dave into the barn, and started scuffling around in the dark.

"You could just borrow a saddle you know, but then you would always have to bring it back. I have an old saddle around here somewhere. Ah here it is!" He lifted it. "This saddle needs a little bit of work, but you can keep it if you want it."

Joseph helped carry the saddle to the sunlight leaking in through the cobweb-covered window. The horn and one stirrup were missing. Dave tipped his hat and scratched his head. "It's probably in there somewhere." He walked back into the shadows with Joseph following.

Joseph spotted the saddle horn. "Here it is! Here's the saddle horn!" His heart beat faster.

"And here is a stirrup you can use, not quite matching, but I think it will work." They walked back into the light where Dave showed Joseph what needed to be done to make the saddle ready for riding again. "Think you can do it?"

"Yes! I think it will work!" Joseph grabbed all the pieces and started for the trail. "Oh, and thank you!"

"Let me know if you need any more help."

Joseph spent the next several days fixing his saddle. He attached all the missing parts and polished and oiled the leather. Then he practiced putting it on Root Beer and riding. He adjusted the stirrups, until everything was just right.

Finally the big day came. Joseph packed his lunch in his backpack. He included some cowboy granola bars, which he'd invented in the kitchen the day before. After saddling Root Beer, he headed out before daylight. He rode to John Wayne's house in the Green Basin and met up with all the other cowboys. The cows milled about in a holding pen, while the riders gathered.

Joseph tied Root Beer to a fence post and joined the other men and boys. As he listened to their stories of roping and branding, he felt like a green horn, but once they opened the gate and started the cattle down the road, he forgot all about that. John Wayne told him to ride along the left side of the cows and help some of the other boys keep the cows out of the ditch on that side.

As the day wore on, Joseph became more confident. Soon he rode along and yelled, "Yah!" with the rest, doing the work of a real cowboy on a real cattle drive.

CHAPTER 13

Drive-Through Donuts and Books

"The driver's coming! The driver's here!"
Rachel started the cry and carried it through the house.
Everybody scrambled to find coats, bonnets, and hats. Ruth
finished the lunch and snacks she was preparing for the road.
Joseph filled the water bottles, while Rebecca firmly pinned the
baby's diaper and slipped the baby's arms into her tiny coat.
They joined the rest of the family and climbed into the van.

They were going to Kalispell for a day of shopping – a rare
day – because the whole family was going to town. What an
exciting adventure!

As the van rolled along around the curves and across the
lake, Rebecca mentally reviewed the places they wanted to go.
The most important stop was Costco to get groceries. Lester
needed bike parts from Wheaton's Bike Shop. The highlight of
the trip would be visiting the used bookstore. The whole family
enjoyed reading books.

When they arrived at the used bookstore, everybody found
their favorite section. Rebecca was left with baby Rosemary.
She found a few books with pasteboard pages, so the baby
couldn't tear them and settled little Rosemary in a corner, while

she quickly scanned the shelves. Her eyes caught the name Catherine Marshall, the author of the book *Christy*. Rebecca liked that book, so she pulled out the Catherine Marshall book and opened it. She scanned the pages. Fifteen minutes later she was startled out of her reverie by Jonathan who tugged on her dress with his persistent voice saying, "Mommy! Mommy! Look! See what the baby just did!"

Rebecca tore her eyes from the printed page to see Jonathan gently take a book from Rosemary's little hand and say, "No, no, you must not do this, no, no."

With a glance to see if anybody else saw them, Rebecca dropped to her knees next to her baby and the piles of books around her. She started placing the books back on the shelf. Rosemary had pulled books off the shelves and piled them in stacks on the floor. Rebecca breathed a sigh of relief when she saw none of them was torn.

"I can look at books with her and watch her," Jonathan said as he chose a picture book and settled on the floor beside his baby sister.

Just then Lester came around the corner and asked, "Are you ready to go? Have you found anything you want?"

Rebecca stared at the shelves of books for a moment like a child in a candy store. She wanted to tell her husband she wouldn't be ready for a couple more hours, but she knew they couldn't keep the driver waiting that long. After she handed the books she had chosen to Lester, she went in search of the children. Ruth clutched a few books she really wanted, and Joseph and Rachel eagerly showed her their selection of books. They all handed their books over to their dad. Ruth picked up the baby, and the small group walked up to the counter to pay.

As they started the ninety-mile journey towards home, Rebecca wished she could read the books she had bought, but she knew better than to read while on the road or she would have to throw up for sure. She already felt queasy. Ever since she was a child, she struggled with carsickness. She closed her eyes and idly listened to her husband chatting with the driver.

"Oh, Mom. Look at that huge donut!" Rachel exclaimed. Rebecca opened her eyes to see what she was talking about. "It says, 'Drive-Through Donuts'!"

Ruth and Joseph exchanged smiles. Rachel's head turned as she kept looking back at the huge lighted donut for as long as she could see it. Five miles down the road, Rachel looked at her mother, took a deep breath, and asked, "Does it really mean they drive through the donuts?"

The seriousness of her expression stirred up a fit of laughter from her siblings. Lester turned and asked, "What's so funny?"

While Ruth and Joseph explained to their dad what they were laughing about, Mother explained it to Rachel. "It means you don't have to get out of your car. You can just drive through and pick up the donuts at the window."

CHAPTER 14

Mint Tea and Forgiveness

The teakettle bubbled and jiggled on the stove, as Rebecca gathered a pen and a couple sheets of notepaper. She settled at the kitchen table with a cup of peppermint tea and relished the sweet aroma of the steaming cup. As she breathed in the refreshing scent, her thoughts drifted back over the book she had just read.

Catherine Marshall had written about her sickness and depression. She couldn't shake it until she learned how to truly forgive the people who had wronged her in life. The book provided a clear reminder. *Jesus taught that we need to forgive people if we want to be forgiven by God.* Rebecca hadn't thought of it like that before. But it was true. *Instead of holding on to grudges and unforgiveness, I need to forgive people.*

She wrapped her fingers around the cup of hot tea, enjoyed the warmth, and contemplated whom she needed to forgive from her past. Breathing a prayer for guidance, she picked up her pen and began to write. She filled one page and then another. First, she wrote the name of the person, followed by the offense. She recalled any hurtful words that still stuck in her head and came to mind when she thought of the person who said them. She added people who had done something that hurt her as well as people who had hurt her by not doing what they should have and even the times she'd been hurt by being left out or forgotten. The list grew as her pen scratched across the paper.

Some were major life-altering incidents. Others were so minor she almost dismissed them, but to her way of thinking, if it was significant enough that she still remembered it, she needed to forgive and let it go.

After an hour of intense writing, she took a deep breath and leaned back in her chair. Her tea had cooled, but her heart had grown warmer.

She went back to the beginning of her list and prayed out loud. "Lord, I forgive _____ for (name the incident) to me. I forgive _____ and bless _____ in Jesus's name." She went down the list and prayed for each individual. One at a time she prayed the prayer of forgiveness and blessing. When she finally finished, she breathed a prayer of thanks, and she wadded the papers up in a ball. She opened the top lid of the kitchen range and tossed them in. As the paper went up in smoke, her heart filled with lightness and relief. It was equal to the time she'd asked God to forgive her sins and asked Jesus to be her Savior.

With a new spring to her step, Rebecca refilled her cup with hot tea from the back of the stove and headed for the quilt.

CHAPTER 15

Art Lessons

One Saturday Joseph rode his bicycle up the hill toward Border Lumber on his way to Homer's cabin for art lessons. In his backpack, he carried a few of his art treasures – the primary colors and black and white acrylic paints and a few brushes, including his favorite fan brush.

The mill stood quiet as he rode along the dusty lane to Bachelor Hill. He turned up the trail away from the mill and slowed down. The cabin was somewhere along here on the left, but he wasn't quite sure which one it was. Then he spotted Homer outside waiting for him.

Homer greeted him with a smile. "Looks like you found me."

Joseph followed him inside the cabin, where the kitchen took up one side and the living room the other. A ladder led up to the loft overhead. An odd mixture of kitchen furniture, saddles, guns, beds, chairs, and camping gear decorated the place. Marion and Eli had said some of the bachelors had guitars, so Joseph looked around for evidence of one. He noticed something that looked electric, but he wasn't sure what it was. It thrilled him to be inside a bachelor's home!

"Mom said you could give me an art lesson?" Joseph said

timidly. He spotted Homer's bow and arrows and scanned the mounts of wild animals on the walls.

Homer didn't say much, while he moved things around by a cabinet next to the couch. He opened it and pulled out some paints and brushes. Joseph shrugged his backpack from his shoulders to take out his own supplies.

Homer set up his supplies on a small table. "I can probably show you some of what I do. I mostly paint things I see in nature."

For the next hour, Joseph watched Homer paint a sunset above a valley in the mountains. His techniques differed from Anna Marie's, the first art teacher he had. Joseph felt like he was in a different world. The smell of leather filled the cabin, and he found the movement of Homer's brush fascinating.

Then it was Joseph's turn. He squeezed some paint out, dipped his brush, and began painting. Homer gave him a few tips on what colors he'd used. Joseph started with the same broad strokes he had seen Homer use. After half an hour, Joseph really liked the way the painting was turning out. Homer went outside to tinker with something, and Joseph kept painting.

When he started painting the mountains though, he ran into trouble. The color he chose for the mountains made his sky look wrong, so he went back to working on the sky. He tried a different color, but that made it worse. The yellow mingled with the blue and turned his sky green. He looked at Homer's painting and saw hints of green in his sky, but it looked good. Discouragement started to rob him of his joy, and he began to feel irritated.

Homer stepped into the cabin and walked over to see how the painting was going. Joseph froze. In frustration, he had just painted an ugly mark diagonally across his sky with bluish green paint. Homer looked at the painting for a moment, then turned and went back outside without saying a word. Joseph refocused on his work. Fifteen minutes later he had repainted the entire sky and decided imperfect was better than doing nothing. He adjusted the mountain color and kept painting.

Homer came back inside and moved around the kitchen. "You want lunch?"

Joseph looked up and nodded his head without saying a word. He felt quite grown up and like a bachelor; he communicated without talking. A few minutes later he joined Homer at the table. They ate sauerkraut and sausage. If his mom had served sauerkraut at home, Joseph would have been disgusted, but here in the bachelor cabin, it was delicious.

After lunch, Joseph brought his painting over and showed it to Homer. "Looking good," he said. He pointed out the green in Joseph's meadows. "Add a little black in that area and it will look better."

After working a while longer, Joseph felt quite pleased with his work. He thanked Homer, loaded up his bicycle, and headed home to show his painting to his family. From this point on, Joseph thought of himself as an artist.

A week later, when Joseph asked if they could have sauerkraut for lunch sometime, his mother looked quite perplexed.

CHAPTER 16

Seekers

Rebecca paused in the bedroom doorway and surveyed the busy scene before her. She tucked her dress in properly and pinned it firmly in place. With one last glance at her sleeping baby in the crib, she quickened her step and joined the woman at the kitchen table to explain to her how she used the sad irons to weigh down the pattern while she marked around them. "Then you remove the pattern to cut the material."

The woman wanted to learn how to make coats for her children, so Rebecca had offered to help her. "Why can't I just pin the pattern to the material and cut around it that way?" the woman asked. Rebecca sighed inwardly.

"Mom, Mom." Rachel, her middle daughter, interrupted her train of thought. "May I take this on the trampoline?" She firmly clutched the gallon jar of cream in her hands. "That way we can all help make butter? I'll be very careful." Her eager eyes pleaded for a yes.

Before she could answer, Ruth, her oldest daughter, called from the kitchen. "Mom, it's important to always measure the oil for the granola first before the honey, isn't it?" It seemed her daughter had a similar dilemma, as she stood at the kitchen counter and explained how to make granola to another woman.

Rebecca nodded to Rachel who hurried out the door, followed by a bunch of youngsters. Then she turned to Ruth. "Yes, if you use the cup to measure the oil first, then the honey just slides out and isn't such a sticky mess."

She turned back to the woman at her side. "I use these patterns over and over again. Using pins every time would cause the patterns to become worn and frayed. Or I might accidentally cut into the patterns, if I cut the material while it's attached to the pattern."

After using the patterns for all her own children, she wanted to pass them on to her daughters someday. In order to preserve her patterns, she used knives or other suitable objects as weights to hold them in position while she traced around them with chalk. Then she removed the pattern and cut along the lines with a pair of sharp scissors.

These women, whom Rebecca referred to as Seekers, wanted to learn how to sew Amish clothes, cook, and make their own food. In other words, they wanted to learn the Amish ways. Some of them wanted to join the Amish church.

Time and again she explained how to do something, but the question would be asked, "Why?"

"Why do you do it this way?"

Sometimes it was very obvious why a thing should be done a certain way, but other times, she herself wondered, "Why indeed?"

She wanted to say, "My mother and grandmother always did it this way." But then she questioned herself. Did it really matter how it was done if the results were the same?

"Why can't you just use a nursing cover while you nurse the baby instead of wearing a cape all the time?"

"Because that's the church rule." There was no other answer.

"And why can't they be different?"

"Because the Bible says we are to have uniformity."

Wait. Does it really say that? She wondered.

After everyone left for the day and she had a moment to herself, she grabbed the Strong's concordance from the shelf and began turning pages. She couldn't find the word *uniformity* in the Bible.

She did find the word *unity* a few times. *Behold, how good and how pleasant it is for brethren to dwell together in unity!* (Psalm 133:1). *Endeavoring to keep the unity of the Spirit in the bond of peace* (Ephesians 4:3). *Till we all come to the unity of the faith and of the knowledge of the Son of God, to a perfect man, to the measure of the stature of the fullness of Christ* (Ephesians 4:13).

It reminded her of a verse Lester had read to her earlier that week.

You search the Scriptures, for in them you think you have eternal life; and these are they which testify of Me. But you are not willing to come to Me that you may have life (John 5:39-40).

"Are we really not coming to Jesus?" she asked herself. "Or are we coming to Jesus to find the rules? Just having rules is a dead thing. There's no life there. I believe this would be an example of what the Scripture means when it says *for the letter kills, but the Spirit gives life*" (2 Corinthians 3:6).

As she pondered all this, all she could think was – *We get so busy trying to make the outside look the same that we neglect the inside.*

Washing Windows

Rebecca smiled at the vigor Marie put into washing windows. She was one of the seekers who wanted to join the Amish church. The old-fashioned remedies and cleaning methods she learned from the Amish women intrigued her. This was her first time to use vinegar water to wash windows, and she enthusiastically touted how sparkling and streak-free the glass became.

Church services were scheduled to be held at Rebecca's house, so the ladies of the neighborhood had gathered to help clean. She settled in the rocking chair to feed the baby and watched Marie diligently wash windows; her thoughts drifted to another time when the subject of washing windows came up.

Two years earlier, Lester and Rebecca had traveled to a settlement where they heard the people lived in unity and love. They'd been told this church based all its rules and regulations on the Bible. They said, "Every rule is supported by Scripture." Lester and Rebecca were very interested and decided to check it out for themselves.

The bishop and his wife were friendly and welcomed Lester and Rebecca into their home. They willingly sat down to go over the *Ordnungs Brief* with them.

As Rebecca scanned the detailed rules written about the house, a line caught her attention. It said the windows of the house were not to be one big pane of glass but were to have a specified number of dividers in each window. The window didn't actually have to be made up of smaller panes but had to look like it did. This was done by using false dividers.

Rebecca waited for a pause in the conversation. When the bishop looked at her, she asked, "Where in the Bible did you find Scripture to regulate the size of the window panes?"

The bishop chuckled and said, "Oh, that is to keep the women busy cleaning those extra corners in the smaller panes; it keeps them out of mischief, so they don't have so much time to gossip and stir up strife."

Rebecca thought of the endless tasks Amish women faced every day and every season. For this man to make light of it and say he would in fact make life a little harder for them by his man-made rules did not sound biblical at all. And that wasn't the only thing that wasn't biblical in that *Ordnungs Brief*. It was just one example.

She thought about Colossians 2:8.

> *Beware lest anyone cheat you through philosophy and empty deceit, according to the tradition of men, according to the basic principles of the world, and not according to Christ.*

Colossians 2:20-23 also came to mind:

> *Therefore, if you died with Christ from the basic principles of the world, why, as though living in the world, do you subject yourselves to regulations – "Do not touch, do not taste, do not handle," which all concern things which perish with the using – according to the commandments and doctrines of men? These things indeed have an appearance of wisdom in self-imposed religion, false humility, and neglect of the body, but are of no value against the indulgence of the flesh.*

They walked away from that settlement feeling subdued and knowing they couldn't move there. They were still searching for the church that would finally get it right.

CHAPTER 17

Deer in the Garden

As Rebecca worked in the garden again, she noticed two loose boards in the garden fence. *I'll have to remind Joseph to bring a hammer and some nails to fix them before the hole gets big enough for a deer to come through.*

She'd seen deer come up to the fence and rub their shoulders on the boards and push against them until they worked them loose in an attempt to get at the lush vegetables growing in the garden. At this late point in the season, there wasn't much left except carrots and cabbage. She gathered the cabbage heads and hoped the deer wouldn't bother the carrots if they did get in. *Although, if they get desperate, I imagine they'd paw up the carrots and eat them too. Maybe the children can dig them up tonight after school.*

She placed a head of cabbage in the bucket and moved on to harvest the next. *If these deer keep eating our vegetables, we need to eat the deer,* she thought to herself. When they first moved to the Kootenai, they thought hunting licenses were too expensive, so they were grateful for the meat others shared with them. Then they learned they could easily get a license for one deer per person, and possibly two. That sounded like a lot of meat.

Most of the men on the Kootenai were avid hunters. But not Lester. Give him a chainsaw or small engine or a sawmill, especially a Wood-Mizer, and there wasn't much he couldn't do; but when it came to hunting, he preferred going to the supermarket.

One year, Rebecca persuaded him to get his tags. She went hunting with him, but it quickly turned into a disaster. A gut shot to a deer further convinced Lester he wasn't meant to be a hunter. He said, "There are other ways to put meat on the table," and his wife agreed with him whole-heartedly, after witnessing that hunting incident.

As soon as Joseph was old enough, they arranged for him to ride with a group of young boys to Eureka for Hunter Safety Training. Rebecca tramped many a mile over the mountains with Joseph to get his tags filled.

Since she had never hunted herself, she talked with Joseph about her getting tags; then he could fill them for her. But she'd trained him too well about living a life of integrity.

He squirmed about it till she said, "Fine, I'll do it myself."

So, this year she had applied for a license and tags for herself. *I wish I could shoot like Annie Oakley*, she thought.

As she carried the buckets full of cabbage to the house, her thoughts wandered to the bachelors who came to West Kootenai for hunting. Most of them couldn't afford a non-resident license. That's why they rented cabins, got jobs, and lived there six months of the year; then they could get resident licenses.

Be Sure of Your Target

Fire crackled in the stove on this chilly day. The older children were at school, and Rebecca sat at the quilt and enjoyed the quiet. Jonathan glanced up from the book he was looking at on the couch. "Mommy, I hear somebody coming."

She listened. Footsteps. They came up onto the porch,

followed by a quick knocking on the door. She raised her voice, "Come in."

A young man stepped inside and carefully closed the door behind him. He stood there and nervously removed his gloves and twisted them in his shaking hands. He breathed hard, as if he'd been running. "I'm in trouble. Can you help me?" He pleaded in a distressed voice.

Rebecca stood and quickly surveyed him with a glance to see if he'd been hurt or maybe even shot, because he seemed so short of breath. She walked away from the quilt and came towards him. "What's wrong? What happened?" It greatly concerned her to see him so agitated.

Jonathan's book slipped from his fingers, and he rose to his knees in order to see the boy more clearly.

The boy's voice faltered. He took a deep breath to steady himself. "I think I shot the wrong elk."

"What were you hunting for?" Rebecca asked, wondering how she could help him; she was not well versed in the hunting laws.

"I had tags for a cow elk, and I think I shot a young bull elk," he explained. "I thought for sure it was a cow till I pulled the trigger." He gulped and took a deep breath and asked in a desperate pleading voice, "What can I do? What if I have to go to jail for shooting the wrong elk? What should I do? Oh, what should I do?"

"Lord, give me wisdom," Rebecca whispered under her breath. He was one of the younger boys who had recently arrived, so she didn't know him very well. She could see he wasn't a wild or bad boy at heart. She wanted to reassure him that it would be all right. But she wasn't sure how serious this was.

Her mind raced to find a solution to help him out of his dilemma. She thought of how Joseph had told her about this one man who seemed to consider himself a self-appointed game warden. He was always trying to catch someone breaking the law.

"Did you see anybody else on the mountain?" she asked.

"No, no," he gulped, as he tried to recall for sure.

"Good," she said reassuringly. "The truth will always work best. The best thing you can do is go to a phone booth and call the game warden before anybody else reports you. Just tell him it was an honest mistake, and if there's a fine, then you will pay it. But I don't think you have to worry about going to jail if you don't hide it."

Relief flooded his face as he pulled on his gloves and said, "Thank you. I'm pretty sure the warden's number is in the phone book by the phone." He hurried out the door.

As his footsteps receded in the distance, Jonathan turned to Rebecca with a thoughtful look on his face.

"Would the police really put him in jail for shooting an elk?" he asked in all seriousness.

You Actually Hit It!

Rebecca glanced at the clock. It was almost time for the children to come home from school. She walked to the window where she could see the garden, and she stretched and flexed her tired fingers and wrists. Sure enough, that fat doe was trying to get into the garden again. "Oh, that pesky, persistent deer!" she exclaimed under her breath. "I'll get you yet."

She turned toward the door when she heard the thud-thud of bikes being set against the porch. The children burst in the door with their empty lunch boxes.

"Hey Joseph," she said as she looked out the window again. "That deer is down there again. I'm going to see if I can get it. Will you please load the gun for me?"

Joseph eagerly went for the .30-06 the bachelors had lent them for hunting. He carefully loaded the ammunition, while Rebecca put on an orange hunting vest and checked to see if her tags were in her pocket.

"Okay, let's go," she said as she took the gun and headed for the porch. She crossed the yard and carefully balanced the gun on the rail fence, peering through the sights.

"Lord, please help me now," she breathed. "I don't want to miss."

She scrutinized the area all around the deer. *No other living creature visible.* Gripping the barrel firmly with the left hand, she lined up the deer in the hairline of the sights. Slowly she squeezed the trigger. *Bang!* The shot fired. An instant later the deer dropped to the ground.

"You hit it!" Joseph exclaimed. "You actually killed it!"

"That's what I was aiming for," Rebecca said with a twinkle in her eye. "Thank you, Lord." She leaned against the fence to steady her shaky knees, while she took one more look through the scope to make sure she had hit the deer properly.

With gun in hand, they cautiously approached the deer. It was dead. The shot had gone right through the spinal cord in the neck.

Joseph cut the throat, so it would bleed out properly. Then he removed the glands to keep the meat from having that wild gamey taste.

By the time Lester got home, the deer was gutted and hanging in the woodshed. It would cool off until the next day, when they'd prepare the meat for the freezer and canning. The little Amish-owned store provided freezer space for the community in their generator-cooled freezer unit.

CHAPTER 18

Traditions or Jesus?

Rebecca surveyed the kitchen as she untied her apron and hung it in the pantry. With everything neatly in its place, things were ready for Sunday. The couple who had been there for supper had left, and after the dishes were washed and the house tidied, the children had all gone to bed.

Rebecca walked slowly into the living room, sat heavily on the couch, and leaned her head in her hands. Lester turned from his desk and eyed her with concern. "What's wrong?"

Rebecca looked at him, as she threw her hands out in a hopeless gesture. "These people don't need to learn German. They need to learn about Jesus. Who cares how they make their clothes, if they don't know the first thing about walking in love toward each other as Jesus commands us?"

"But they want to join the Amish church," Lester countered. "And you know they can't become members until they learn German and dress according to the rules of the church."

"Did you see how that man treats his wife?" Rebecca asked. "She could be dead before he learns enough German to understand what the Bible says about how he should treat his wife."

"Oh, come on. Is it that bad?" Lester leaned back in his chair and stroked his beard.

"It's worse." Rebecca rose and walked to the window with her Bible in hand and looked out at the peaceful scene. The moon shone brightly through the tall pine trees and cast long shadows across the yard. It was so bright she could read a book by the light of the moon, and she highly suspected Ruth and Joseph were probably doing just that at their bedroom windows.

"Look at this," she said as she held the open Bible in front of him and pointed at Colossians 2:8.

Beware lest anyone cheat you through philosophy and empty deceit, according to the tradition of men, according to the basic principles of the world, and not according to Christ.

"And here." Her finger slid over to verse 18. "Read from verse 18 to 23 and tell me that isn't talking exactly about our situation in the Amish church," she challenged, as she handed him the Bible and sat on the couch again.

Lester quickly ran his eyes over the Scriptures she had pointed out. "And besides," she went on to say, "some of these people have been divorced and are remarried. You know as well as I do that the Amish church will never accept them as members unless they part from each other. And how ridiculous would that be to tear families apart that are seeking God and wanting what's right?"

"Since when is divorce the unforgivable sin anyway?" she demanded, as her head sank into her hands again.

"You tell me." Lester handed the Bible back to her. "As a preacher, I'm commanded to feed the sheep."

"Right, the Bible says, *Feed my sheep*! Not teach my sheep to speak German," Rebecca declared, opened the Bible again, and flipped pages to the book of Mark.

She found the place she was looking for and said, "Listen to this. Here in Mark chapter 7 verse 7 Jesus is talking, and He says, *In vain they worship Me, teaching as doctrines the commandments of men.*" She cleared her throat, which felt tight with emotion. "Then in verse nine Jesus says, *All too well you reject the commandment of God, that you may keep your tradition.* Also in verse 13 He says, *making the word of God of no effect through your tradition which you have handed down.*"

She looked up into her husband's eyes and said, "That sounds like what we are doing when we are so busy teaching these people they have to cut up their driver's licenses, get rid of their photos, make their clothes just right with so many pins here, so many buttons there, their hat brims just the right width, and then on top of that, learn to speak one dialect of German and read the Bible in another dialect. All before we teach them about salvation."

Lester reached for his Bible. "See what it says here in 1 Peter 1:18," he said. "*Knowing that you were not redeemed with corruptible things, like silver or gold, from your aimless conduct received by tradition from your fathers.*"

"Oh, that's good." Rebecca walked over to see the words with her own eyes. "And read what it says in verses 19 and 21," she said as her eyes scanned quickly down the page.

"Ah, yes," Lester said. "It says we are redeemed with the precious blood of Christ so that our faith and hope are in God."

"And not in our traditions," Rebecca finished. They sat in silence marked by the tick of the clock on the wall. After a long moment passed, Rebecca roused herself out of her reverie and contemplation. She stood. "We need to go to bed if we want to go to church tomorrow."

"We can't solve all the world's problems in one evening," Lester said as he followed suit. "Guess we'll have to take one day at a time and keep seeking God's will."

"The Bible has all the answers to the world's problems, if we weren't so blinded that we couldn't understand them," Rebecca mused half to herself and half out loud.

Why does life have to be so complicated? She wondered as she prepared for bed. Just as she started to drift off to sleep, Lester rolled over and asked, "So, you're suggesting we should start having Bible studies in English?"

Rebecca's eyes popped open, instantly wide awake again. "Shouldn't we? Isn't that what these people really need? If they won't allow us to use English in church and Sunday school, maybe we could just get together here and study the Bible and have prayer with those who are seeking. What could be wrong with that?"

What could be wrong with that indeed?

CHAPTER 19

Bachelor Revival

Rebecca rose from her quilt to check the fire. A glance at the glowing embers sent her to the porch for another chunk of wood. It wasn't bitterly cold, but a steady fire kept the house comfortable for the baby. As she lifted a chunk of wood, a lone biker whizzed up the driveway. She watched him for a moment, as he turned in at the bike shop. *It must be somebody who knows Lester is home from work.*

Convictions

People often dropped by in the evenings for bike repairs, so she thought nothing more of it till later that evening, after the older children were in bed. As she changed the baby's diaper for the night, Lester brought it up.

"That's the third person to come to me this week to ask to make a confession in church to clear his conscience of something he did that broke the church rules."

"What do you think is bringing this about?" Rebecca asked, as she tucked the blankets snugly around the baby.

"I don't know; they just say they are convicted and want to be at peace." Lester paused to slip off his shoes. "Most of them also say they appreciate that I'm their friend and not judging them."

"It's such a long time till communion when the bishop comes out that I don't think it's right or reasonable to make them wait that long to get these things off their chests." Lester climbed into bed. "What would you think about just having a members' meeting and letting them confess this next Sunday?"

"Seems like the Christian thing to do," Rebecca agreed and blew out the lamp.

Confessions

Sunday morning dawned clear and bright. Rebecca relished the peaceful aura of getting ready for church all together rather than rushing off in different directions to get to work and school. When they arrived at the house where church services were being held that day, Rebecca and the girls went to the house, while Lester and the boys joined the men out by the barn.

After shaking hands with the girls standing around in the kitchen, Rebecca found a seat with the women in the living room. *My, there must be a lot of tourists here again*, she thought, as she noted all the different styles of head coverings, capes, and dresses the girls were wearing. There were almost always visitors, which made it harder to get to know the girls who actually lived in that area.

As she settled on the bench behind the older women, Rebecca hid a smile, when the girls filed in and sat behind her. One of the girls was visibly chewing and cracking away on a mouthful of gum. An older girl in black chided her for chewing gum in church. The gum chewer leaned forward to look the girl in black in the eye. "Our church has no rules that we can't chew gum," she told her defiantly.

"Do we need a rule to be respectful?" the older girl asked.

The girls quieted down as the ministers came in, followed by the men and boys.

Lester was preaching today. With so many visiting preachers lately, he often only had the *angfang* (beginning) of the service or an opportunity to give *zeugnisz* (testimony given by the elders).

Rebecca's eyes scanned the crowd of people. She knew many by name, and some she knew by character. A lot of the boys from Bachelor Hill were in attendance. She smiled, as she remembered the conversation she'd heard between two of the older men last Sunday, while she helped wait on the tables after the church service.

"Have you noticed how many of the boys are coming to church regularly now?" one man asked the other.

"Yes, I have and I wonder what's going on," the other said. "I mean, I've been trying to get them to church for so long, and now they're even filling the tables in the singings. They're actually helping sing." They shook their heads in mutual agreement that something must be happening for these wild bachelors to be showing up so regularly for church. What was their motive? Hmmm.

Lester's voice drew her attention back to her present surroundings. After he'd announced where the church services would be held next Sunday, he asked all the members to remain seated. Rebecca handed the baby to Ruth who took her outside where all the non-members went. Just the members were left in the room.

After everyone settled again, Lester announced that in the past week three young men had come to him with requests to be allowed to make a confession before the church and ask for forgiveness for things they had done that were not allowed, according to the rules of the church. He named the three young men and asked them to leave the room, while he took a vote to see if the congregation was willing to accept their confessions.

As the three rose to leave the room, Lester added, "And if there are any others who have something they'd like to get off their consciences, now is a good time to do it. *Now is the day of salvation,*" he quoted (2 Corinthians 6:2).

At a gasp and a whispered exclamation from a girl behind her, Rebecca lifted her eyes to see one after another of the boys and men get up and leave the room. As they filed out, they paused by Lester to tell him what they were confessing. The rest of the church members left in the room sat in stunned silence, because over two benches full of young men left the room.

Lester started to tell the congregation what it was these young men had confessed but gave up and said, "Due to the number of confessions that came forward, I don't want to say something wrong, so I'll just let each one confess in turn. That way I won't get it mixed up."

Everybody seemed agreeable to that, and when nobody raised any objections, the young men were brought back in. One by one they confessed their misdeeds and asked for forgiveness and prayer. Lester commended them for their honesty and encouraged them to stay on track with the Lord as their guide.

When church was dismissed, Rebecca glanced at the older men – especially the two who had been talking about why the bachelors were coming to church and singings. They sat there looking at each other in shock. "What just happened?" Their expression seemed to be asking each other.

"Did we just experience an old-fashioned revival?" Rebecca heard the girl in black ask under her breath.

Most of the people rejoiced in the event that just took place. How wonderful that these young men came in repentance and became upstanding members. However, at least one man was clearly thinking it was time to let the bishop back East know what was going on. Things were getting out of hand with this young preacher doing things only a bishop should be allowed to do.

CHAPTER 20

Spiritual Warfare

Lester came home from work, smelling of sawdust and pine tar. "Have you got a minute?" he asked Rebecca, who was in the kitchen getting supper on the table.

"Always," she said and followed her husband into the living room.

"There's this man coming to a local schoolhouse to speak and teach on spiritual warfare. One of the workers at the mill said he is taking his family, and he invited us to go with them. What do you think?" Lester paused as he studied his wife's face to see if she would be favorable to the idea.

Rebecca felt the eagerness in his voice, and after a moment's thought she said, "If you don't think it will get us in trouble."

"Some of the other Amish are going too," Lester told her.

She answered slowly. "Well, then I don't see why we shouldn't."

So, it was decided. They took the whole family to the meetings. Rebecca sat spellbound, as the man preached and taught what the Bible said about spiritual warfare.

"It's not people who are our enemies," he explained. "It's principalities and powers of darkness. Ephesians 6:12 tells us *we do not wrestle against flesh and blood, but against principalities, against powers, against the rulers of the darkness of this age, against spiritual hosts of wickedness in the heavenly places."*

He explained how some people are actually possessed and controlled by demons, while others are oppressed by demons and powers of darkness. He showed them where the Bible tells to resist the devil and cast out demons. He told stories of people who were possessed, and he explained how they were freed from demonic forces.

After the meetings, Lester and Rebecca went home and cleaned house. Literally and spiritually. They burned papers, books, and anything that pertained to things of darkness.

They prayed over themselves and their children and their belongings, binding any powers of darkness in any way associated or connected with them and casting them out in Jesus's name.

It was a time of cleansing warfare.

Powwowing and Witchcraft (Brauching)

One evening after Lester arrived home from work, he shared some news with Rebecca. "Coming home from work today, I met a neighbor who says some people who were at the spiritual warfare meetings gave him some tapes by a Mennonite man who preaches and teaches more extensively about the practice of witchcraft and *brauching* (placing hands on people and healing them) in the Amish and Mennonite circles. He's inviting some of us to his house to listen to those tapes and learn more about how to be free of bondage."

After discussing it, Lester and Rebecca decided to join the group and listen to this series of teachings. As they listened, their eyes were opened to the evils of some of the practices of *brauching* that had been done in their past.

This man explained how the devil often tried to appear as an angel of light – how he likes to imitate good spiritual things. Even when people practice devil worship and get their requests granted by the devil, he gets the best end of the deal. It's usually a trade-off, because it gives the devil a foothold in their lives.

As Rebecca listened to this man's teachings that exposed dark practices within the Amish, her mind strayed back to her childhood. When she was six years old, her family traveled from Missouri to Iowa to visit her grandparents on her mother's side of the family. It was summertime, and one afternoon her two single aunts and older cousins were working in the garden. A bunch of the cousins had gathered for the day at Grandpa's, and Rebecca played with them in the yard.

All at once, she heard her name being called by her aunts. She went to see what they wanted but drew back in alarm when she saw the dirty little creature one aunt held. With all the cousins crowding around, the aunts explained it was a mole. They'd hoed it up while it was making a burrow in the garden.

"And," they explained excitedly, "if you hold a mole in your hands till it dies, then you'll have the power to *brauch*. But you have to do it before you are seven years old, or it won't work."

"I, I don't want to touch it," Rebecca protested as she backed away. "Let someone else do it."

"Oh no, you're so close to seven that this will probably be your last chance," they argued. "Wouldn't you like to be able to heal people and make little babies feel better?"

"Not if I have to hold that nasty thing." Rebecca tried to squirm free of the circle crowding around her.

But her aunts took hold of her and led her to a grassy spot. "Sit down," they said. They went on to assure her they would stay with her, and they placed the squirmy, nasty little creature of darkness into her hands.

At first all the cousins gathered around to watch this novelty, but soon they lost interest and ran off. Stiffly and uncomfortably, Rebecca sat there holding the mole. It seemed hours before the aunts pronounced it dead. How relieved she was to get rid of it and go scrub her hands. She thought she could wash it off and forget it. She thought she could go back to being just another little Amish girl. But some things go deeper than the skin. Much deeper.

After that traumatic incident, Rebecca could take a fussy baby and hold it snugly against her stomach, which caused the baby to quiet down almost instantly. But as this happened, she experienced pains in her stomach. Or if the baby had an earache, and she placed her hand over the baby's ears, she soon experienced pain in her ears while the baby calmed down and drifted peacefully off to sleep.

While this ability to "heal" became obvious to those around her, the healing came with consequences – consequences Rebecca couldn't seem to share with anybody. As a little girl who didn't see the connection to the incident with the mole, she had no clue what caused them or how to get rid of them.

Nightmares

After that incident, Rebecca also had nightmares – unearthly nightmares that caused her to shiver and pull the covers up over her head. Night after night these horrible dreams plagued her until she dreaded going to bed. To feel safer, she always chose to sleep in the middle of the bed between her sisters or with her back against the wall.

Whenever she tried to tell her mother about the dreams, the words stuck in her throat, and she couldn't get them out. She couldn't even tell her sister Katie about the awful things she dreamed. They told each other everything else, but for some reason, she couldn't tell her about the nightmares.

As time went on, Rebecca learned to tuck the dreams in the back of her mind during the day and pretend everything was all right. But at odd moments, all at once, the thoughts flooded in to petrify her. When this happened, she almost couldn't function.

As she got older, she learned to cover these moments up with talking and laughing and telling stories to make others laugh or to entertain her younger brothers and sisters. She filled her spare moments with reading. If she could get her hands on a good book, she could lose herself in the story and forget the horrible nightmares.

Then one in-between Sunday when they didn't go to church (church services were only held every other Sunday), her dad gathered everybody in the living room after breakfast. As was his custom on the Sundays when there was no church, he told them to get their New Testaments, and they all took turns reading. This excited Rebecca, because she'd just recently been allowed to take her turn to read a verse. She already knew how to read English, but this was German. Her dad coached them along as each brother and sister and Mother and Dad took turns reading a verse at a time. After the Bible reading, they got the German songbooks, and Dad encouraged everybody to choose a song and lead it. If they needed help to start it, his voice would be right there helping them along.

Rebecca loved to sing – especially when she could sing with her dad. After the singing, Dad pulled out the German spelling book and pronounced the German words. The children took turns spelling. This helped them learn the sounds and words better.

On this particular Sunday, after they were done spelling, her dad reached for another little green German book. Grandpa and Grandma had given all the grandchildren one of these, so Rebecca had her own copy. It had the German alphabet and little lessons in German reading. In the back of the book was the Lord's Prayer in German and some other little prayers written in rhyming words.

Dad told the children, "I want you all to memorize the Lord's Prayer by the next Sunday." Memorizing enthralled Rebecca, and the little prayers written in rhyme intrigued her. Her dad explained what they meant, so she memorized two of them.

> O lieber Heiland, Jesus Christ,
>> Der du für Kinder kommen bist,
> Wollst in mein Herz heut kehren ein,
>> Wollst deines Schäfleins Hirte sein! Amen.

> (O Beloved Savior, Jesus Christ
>> Because you have come for children too
> Wilt live in my heart today
>> Wilt be your lamb's shepherd true. Amen.)

And the other prayer on the last page of the book:

> Lieber Gott, nun schlaf ich ein,
>> Schicke mir ein Engelein,
> Lasz es bei dem Bette stehen
>> Und nach meinen Herzen sehn,
> Dasz es werde gänzlich rein,
>> Wie es musz im Himmel sein. Amen.

> (Beloved God, now I go to sleep
>> Send me an angel
> Let it stand by my bed.
>> To watch over my heart
> So it can be completely pure
>> As it has to be in heaven. Amen.)

That evening when Rebecca got in bed, she prayed that prayer. And lo and behold, when she woke up the next morning, she felt refreshed. She didn't have a single bad dream. What a relief!

After that, she prayed that prayer every night asking God to send His angels to watch over her to protect her from nightmares.

In the morning, she prayed the prayer about Jesus being in her heart. Soon she started feeling the presence of His protection, and she added her own words to the prayers. Anytime of the day, when she felt afraid or troubled, she prayed. God truly looked after His little lamb, and she was one happy child.

Mother's Death

But then she experienced a death, and that changed things again. The summer Rebecca turned ten her mother started getting sick spells. She went to the doctor, and he gave her some medicine, but she kept getting worse. Then one Sunday her pains intensified. She tossed and moaned and groaned on her bed. The boys hurried to the neighbors to call the doctor. The doctor came to the house, and after examining her, he said he'd better take her to the hospital.

Later, at the hospital, Rebecca sat in the waiting room with her sisters. The janitor whistled cheerily, as he mopped the hallway. The smell of medicine and floor cleaner hung heavy in the air. The doctor walked in and spoke to her dad in the opposite corner of the room. Rebecca heard bits and pieces. "Exploratory surgery … stomach cancer … spread like wildfire …" Rebecca tried to hear more. Her imagination ran wild. How did cancer look when it spread that fast? It was like one of her nightmares. She needed the images in her head to stop. She tried to pray. The janitor kept whistling, as he moved further down the hallway. A door opened somewhere, and she got a whiff of the heavy smell of sickness.

When Rebecca returned home, she prayed like she had never prayed before. She begged and pleaded that the Lord would heal her mother. What made it worse was that just a couple months before, her best friend's mother had died suddenly of a blood clot on the brain. Rebecca had seen the pain and grief her friend's family had gone through, losing a mother with ten children left behind.

In spite of Rebecca's prayers, after nine days in the hospital, her mother died, leaving behind ten motherless children from ages three to eighteen. Rebecca felt so let down that God hadn't healed her mother. She decided He didn't hear her prayers after all, and she quit praying altogether.

The nightmares came back in full force and worse. She decided that maybe He did hear some prayers, and in sheer self-preservation, she started praying again.

CHAPTER 21

Baptism

At age fifteen, Rebecca read a book titled *The Prince of the House of David*. She'd tried reading it when she was much younger but got bogged down with it. This time it came alive. It was the story of a young girl living with her cousins Lazarus, Mary, and Martha during the last three years of the life of Jesus. This girl wrote letters to her father and gave a day-by-day account of the happenings around Jesus during his ministry and crucifixion.

For the first time, Rebecca began to understand why Jesus had suffered and died. She'd prayed that prayer as a child and asked Jesus to come into her heart, which had been a step in the right direction. Now she prayed and asked Jesus to forgive her sins and be her Savior. She began to read the Bible with new understanding even though it was in German.

When she read Mark 16:16, which says, *He who believes and is baptized will be saved*, she went to her dad and told him she wanted to be baptized. Her dad looked troubled. He said, "You'll have to wait a couple more years till you're seventeen." The church wouldn't allow her to get baptized this young.

For two years, she lived with the fear of death hanging over her head. The devil taunted her with thoughts like, "If you die now, you'll go to hell. You've reached the age of accountability, so you better get baptized before you die." Finally, the church allowed her to join the baptism class during the summer she was seventeen.

Each Sunday morning, while the rest of the congregation sang the slow-paced songs from the *Ausbund*, Rebecca and the one other girl in the class followed the bishop and ministers to another room, the *Abroth*, where they went through a segment of the lessons required to become eligible for baptism in the Amish church.

The last Sunday of classes the bishop told them that the congregation would have a members' meeting right after church (before lunch) to take a vote to see if everybody agreed that the two girls were ready to be baptized.

When the church dismissed them, Rebecca filed out with the other girls and stood under the shade trees in the front yard and waited for the outcome. After a while, the deacon and one of the ministers came out and motioned to Rebecca. With knees shaking, she followed them to the side of the yard where they told her that it had been brought to their attention that she had a pin in the back of her collar that was against the *Ordnung* of the church. Feeling like a criminal convicted of a serious crime, Rebecca's throat went so dry she could hardly speak. Her hands trembled so much that she could barely remove the offending pin to show that she was willing to comply with the rules.

After the ministers went back to report to the congregation that she had corrected the offense, Rebecca went to the outdoor toilet to compose herself – away from all the eyes she felt were staring at her. Everybody knew that you must have done something bad if the ministers had to talk to you.

As Rebecca tried to choke back the tears and control her emotions, her mind raced. Why had nobody ever told her it was wrong all those other Sundays? She had always put a pin in there to hold the fold of her cape in place, so she didn't have to worry about it coming apart. Surely, someone had seen it and could have mentioned it to her, instead of waiting and making such a scene of it.

The Saturday before the day she was to be baptized, she was to attend another class where the ministers would go through the eighteen articles of the Dortrecht Confession of Faith with the applicants. It was such a pleasant day Rebecca decided to walk to the class. As she walked along the side of the road, she enjoyed the sound of the birds in the trees along the fencerows. It felt good to be alive. She looked forward to getting baptized, so she wouldn't have the fear of going to hell if she died. When she approached the bishop's house, the preachers stood in the front yard. As she passed them, they paused in their conversation and then resumed talking when she went inside to take off her bonnet and greet the bishop's wife.

Soon the men came in, and they spent the next few hours going over the Articles of Faith. These articles had been adopted and signed in 1632 by the brethren in Holland. The Amish had made a tradition of always requiring their members to read these before baptism.

Later that day as Rebecca sat by her upstairs window, enjoying the cool evening breeze, she heard the clip-clop of a horse on the road, accompanied by the rattling of buggy wheels. The buggy slowed and turned into their driveway. In the evening shadows, she saw her dad go out to meet the men in the buggy. The voices of the ministers grew louder and louder. The bishop was a kindly, godly, older man with a hearing problem, so he couldn't hear what the other ministers said unless they raised their voices.

As Rebecca heard and comprehended what the men said to her dad, she moved away from the window, but what she'd heard made her feel sick to the stomach. She thought these men had been chosen by God Himself to be preachers. Surely, they were holy men to be revered. Now she was shocked and shaken to the core of her being because of how human and petty they really were. They were picking on her dad, trying to get him in trouble for the smallest things. Her spirit felt bruised and betrayed. Tears brimmed and spilled down her cheeks, and they just kept coming. She felt as if she could never stop crying.

The next morning while getting ready for church, she struggled to hold back her tears, which caused a painful lump in her throat. Once at church in the *abroth,* tears overwhelmed her again when she thought about the things these men had said to her dad. She struggled to control herself, but the tears kept coming. She thought the ministers probably wondered what was wrong with her, but she couldn't help herself. Looking back later, she thought it must've grieved the Holy Spirit so much that it just overflowed in tears.

Years later the bishop wrote a letter to Rebecca and apologized to her for the way things went that week. Rebecca had nothing but the highest respect for him.

Now that the day she'd looked forward to for so long finally arrived, the relief she expected to feel after being baptized was clouded by the dawning realization of the fallacy of the system of the Amish church. Baptism should be a time of rejoicing, not a time of increased fears.

As she grew older, Rebecca struggled with all kinds of fears as she clung to her prayers. Some days it seemed as if she had to pray all day just to get through. Her worst fear was that her dad would get sick and die too.

Sitting in the group of neighbors and listening to the cassette tapes of the man teaching about the superstitions and dark practices of the Amish, Rebecca thought back to all the days and years she'd struggled with all those fears. Fears of not being good enough to go to heaven. Fears of dying or her dad dying. Fears of what the devil might do to her. But what the devil had intended for evil had actually started her to rely on prayer and constantly look to God for deliverance. She had learned Whom to look to for help, but she had yet to learn to trust.

Now, after hearing this man teach on the evils of *brauching*, she knew what she had to do. She prayed, binding and casting out that evil, demonic spirit of fear that had entered her soul when she held that filthy mole to death so many years before as an innocent child.

Dear Heavenly Father,

Thank you for redeeming me from the curse. In the name of Jesus, I command all evil spirits and powers of darkness to leave me. I plead the blood of Jesus over myself. I am free because Jesus set me free. Praise you and thank you, Lord. Amen.

Rebecca didn't feel an instant difference, but as time went on, she experienced a new freedom in her spirit. The fearful thoughts didn't have power to depress her anymore. She had a new joy in her heart.

CHAPTER 22

God Is Love

J oseph shifted on the hard, wooden bench and tried to find a comfortable position as his dad rose to preach. He idly focused on a fly that buzzed on the windowpane beside him. He inched his cupped hand closer to see if he could capture the distraught fly. Just as he was about to make the catch, his hand stopped in midair. He glanced at the faces of the men in front of him. Were they hearing what he was hearing? One of the men shuffled his feet; another shifted his position and cleared his throat.

His dad spoke in English. Joseph hadn't caught what he said leading up to it because his attention had been on the fly, but now his dad was quoting from a song in English:

> The love of God is greater far
>   Than tongue or pen can ever tell,
> It goes beyond the highest star
>   And reaches to the lowest hell. . . .
>
> Could we with ink the ocean fill,
>   And were the skies of parchment made,

> Were every stalk on earth a quill,
> And every man a scribe by trade;
> To write the love of God above
> Would drain the ocean dry,
> Nor could the scroll contain the whole,
> Though stretched from sky to sky.[1]

At the end of the verse, his dad spoke in German again and explained how much God really loves us – enough to send His Son Jesus to die for us. Joseph let out a long breath and turned his attention to the fly. He hadn't realized he was holding his breath till his dad started speaking in German again. With the fly gone, Joseph turned his full attention back to his dad. Maybe it wasn't such a big deal to speak English if quoting a song.

In the past, Joseph had heard some of the men discuss the reason they couldn't allow English to be used in church services. "We would lose the old ways," they said. "If we lose the old ways, everything will soon be lost. So we must stick to the old ways at all costs." And preaching in German was one of those old ways.

When it was time for devotions the next morning at school, Teacher John opened the Bible and read a couple verses. Then he said, "Just like the preacher said yesterday, 'The Love of God' is bigger than we can ever comprehend."

Joseph sat up straight in his chair. If Teacher John repeated what his dad said in church, that gave him reassurance that it was all right. Surely nobody had been offended by the use of the English language, if Teacher John thought it was good. It also felt good that his dad had said something so significant that it was being referred to by the teacher.

---

1   Hymn: "The Love of God," words by Frederick M. Lehman (1917).

CHAPTER 23

A Noise in the Night

I t was butchering day at the Grabers. In the spring, they had bought fifty broiler chicks, and now several neighbors and one of the seeker families had come over to help butcher them. Rebecca had learned about a new way to kill the chickens that would bleed them better without being as bruised, so today they replaced the chopping block with cones. Other than that, it was the same process they'd used for years, and Rebecca enjoyed instructing the beginners.

By nightfall they'd butchered all the chickens. The meat cooled in tubs in the washhouse until they could process it in the morning. The washhouse was an enclosed porch at the front of the house. It offered a nice secure place to store things, except for the fact that one of the doorknobs had broken and been removed but not replaced. Rebecca solved that problem by borrowing a bungee strap from Lester's bike shop. The neighbors had recently shot the mountain lion that had caused problems in the area, so she wasn't too worried. But just in case something did try to get in, she tested the door. It would take quite a push to open it. *That should be good enough*, Rebecca thought as she went in to start supper.

Later that evening, as the day wound down, Lester closed his Bible and prepared for bed. Rebecca stitched a final row in the quilt and went to make sure the children were sleeping in their beds. Joseph was sprawled on the couch, reading. He'd been introduced to the writings of Harold Bell Wright and read through those books every spare moment he had.

"Don't stay up too late." Rebecca paused in the doorway. "And be sure to turn off the light when you go to bed." He grunted that he'd heard her, and soon the house settled for the night. The only sounds were the hum of the gas light, the ticking of the clock, and the sound of the pages turning. Other than that, silence of the night settled in.

Suddenly, a sound from outside invaded that silence. *Streeetch. Bang!* Joseph lifted his head, shot to a sitting position, and listened. *Shuffle, shuffle. Streeetch, bang! Shuffle, shuffle.*

It sounded like it came from the porch. He set his book down and looked for a flashlight. The scuffling sound continued on the front porch. He inched toward the door and looked through the window in the door. Then he flipped the switch on the flashlight. Two feet from his face the beady eyes and snout of a bear looked back at him!

In that moment, the only thing he could think of was his mother saying, "Next time a bear comes around, make sure I see it! Don't scare it until I've seen it!"

Joseph raced for the bedroom. "Mom, Mom!" he whispered urgently.

Rebecca sat up. "What?"

"There's a bear on the front porch," Joseph whispered excitedly.

"Really?" Rebecca's bare feet padded across the floor to join her son, and they silently headed for the front porch door.

In the bedroom, Lester woke with a start. What had he just heard? Something about the front porch? Rebecca's side of the bed was empty. His feet hit the floor with a thud that shook the house as he came bounding into the living room. Before Rebecca or Joseph made it to the front door, he opened it, strode out onto the porch, and exclaimed loudly, "What's going on? What did you say?"

Rebecca and Joseph looked at each other and burst out laughing. The suspense of the moment had been broken so suddenly that it left them almost hysterical.

"What was it? What's so funny? What are you laughing at? Why aren't you in bed?" This last question Lester directed at Joseph.

"There was a bear, right where you're standing!" Joseph peered into the darkness.

"Yes, it woke me up, and I couldn't figure out what was making such a strange noise," Rebecca added.

"I looked out the window, and it was right here, so I went to tell Mom so she could see it too – and there it is!" Joseph pointed across the driveway where they could see a black bear peering back at them. Illuminated by the beams of their flashlights, the bear turned and went past the root cellar and on up the mountain.

"I really don't see anything funny about a bear trying to break into our house," Lester said as he eyed the now straight faces of his wife and son.

"Can we close the door better so it's more secure, if he comes back or tries again?" Rebecca asked.

Joseph laughed. "He's probably still running, as scared as he was of the ruckus he heard in here."

"Well, let's take a look at the chicken meat." Lester grabbed a flashlight and headed to the washhouse.

"After all that work of raising and butchering those broilers, I don't want to risk losing the meat." Rebecca followed her husband through the door with Joseph bringing up the rear. "I'd say let's move the tubs of meat into the kitchen," she said.

"But with the water, they're so heavy. And the meat needs to be in water."

The beam of her flashlight caught something red on the porch. "Look, the bear must have gotten into that box of apples." Rebecca shone her light on the apples strewn across the porch and onto the lawn. She gathered up the apples and set the box inside, while Lester and Joseph tied the door more securely and barred it on the inside.

"There, I don't think a black bear can get in now," Lester said. "Hopefully no grizzly will even think of trying."

Silence fell over the Graber house once more. All the lights were shut off, and this time everyone got into their beds and settled down.

But sleep didn't come readily for Rebecca. As she lay there listening to her husband's even breathing, as he slumbered, her thoughts went to other nights when she would wake up and couldn't sleep.

Tonight she wasn't awake because she was worried or scared. She felt a great peace and thankfulness that she hadn't been scared to get out of bed and venture out into the night to investigate. Gratitude towards her heavenly Father for sending His only Son, Jesus, to redeem and deliver her from that awful bondage of fear filled her heart with such joy that she wanted to get up and sing. But she refrained. She didn't want to startle her husband again because he needed his sleep. He put in long days of hard work to provide for them all.

As she thought back over all the fears she'd battled as a child and even as a married woman, she marveled at how free she was now. She was no longer scared of the dark, just some of the things in it. She smiled to herself as she drifted off to sleep.

CHAPTER 24

Of Birds

Rebecca pushed her chair away from the quilt and slowly rose to her feet. She rubbed her lower back, straightened her shoulders, then stretched and yawned as she walked over to stir up the fire in the living room heater.

"Look Mommy," Jonathan said from his perch on the windowsill behind his dad's desk. "There are different birds at the feeder, and I'm finding them in the book." He struggled to balance himself while he leafed through Joseph's huge Audubon Bird Book.

"Here." Rebecca reached up to get the smaller bird book from the shelf. "Why don't you use this one? You could certainly handle it better."

"But that's the outdoors one, and I'm indoors now." Jonathan gripped the big book in an effort to keep it balanced on his skinny little knees.

"I know," Rebecca said. "But Joseph wants to keep this book looking nice, and you need to remember that it always belongs on this desk. That way you won't tear it when you look at it."

She gently took the big book and handed Jonathan the smaller one. "This big book cost a bunch of money. Joseph worked hard to save up to buy it, so we need to take good care of it."

"The trampoline cost the most money," Jonathan said, as he looked longingly out the window. "Maybe we can jump on it when Rachel gets home from school."

When they lived on the chicken farm in Puxico, Missouri, the children had pooled their money till they had enough to buy a trampoline. After that, they each bought some books. Joseph chose to get the Audubon books. Ruth and Joseph were both making lists of birds they saw. Here in the West, the birds were different, which raised a new challenge to see who could discover the most new birds.

One difference – no cardinals here. The brilliant red of a cardinal on a green pine tree against a background of pure white snow created a picture that satisfied something deep in Rebecca's soul. While she loved the beauty of the cardinals, in her opinion the melodious warbling trills of the Tennessee Wood Thrush surpassed all other bird songs. But here in Montana, she admired the lovely sheen of the shimmering blue of the Stellar Jays' feathers, and the chickadees were friendly little bundles of feathers. Joseph had proved to them that if you had enough patience to sit motionless on the porch railing with birdseed in your hand, they even ate out of your hand.

The Tennessee woods were full of birds singing and squirrels chattering, while here in Montana the woods seemed so quiet. The Gray Jays could be noisy enough, and there were squirrels here, but a thick layer of pine needles carpeted the ground, and the vastness of the forests and altitude of the mountains muffled sounds. Now Rebecca understood more the title of a book she had once read, *The Silence of the North,* which was an autobiography of a woman who lived in the Canadian woods. Rebecca guessed the Canadian woods were a lot like the Montana woods.

One of Jonathan's favorite spots after his afternoon nap was at the big window where he could watch the birds at the feeder, which hung on the porch outside the window. From there, he also kept an eye out for his siblings coming home from school.

"Here comes Ruth," he said joyfully as he hopped off the desk, onto the chair, then to the floor. He hit the floor running to welcome his siblings and rummage through their lunch boxes to see if they'd left any tasty tidbits for him.

Joseph walked in last and went straight for his bird book to check the description of a bird he'd seen by the lakes.

As they all gathered around the kitchen table for a snack of milk and cookies, Rebecca announced, "We need to get all our chores done quickly, so we're ready to leave when Dad comes home. We have a supper invitation." It was Friday evening, so it didn't matter if they got to bed later, as there was no school the next day.

Everybody scurried to get the work done. They gathered eggs and stacked the wood on the porch in happy anticipation of an evening with friends.

CHAPTER 25

Old Wine

After supper, Lucy shooed the girls out of the kitchen. "You take care of the babies and little ones, and you won't have to help wash dishes." The girls didn't have to be told twice, and the men and boys needed no urging to get out of the kitchen either. That left Lucy and Rebecca alone to visit, as they cleaned up. Rebecca washed dishes, while Lucy put up the food.

Rebecca was glad Lucy was a conversationalist, because she usually had a difficult time talking with strangers. Lucy told Rebecca how she and her husband had met and how thankful she was for a man who was bold in his faith – a man who could lead the family in devotions and teach their boys by word and actions how to live a godly life. Lucy's voice broke.

Rebecca paused in scrubbing the kettle in her dishpan and turned to face her friend. Lucy walked over to her and said softly and confidentially with tears in her eyes, "Don't ever make the mistake I did."

"What do you mean? What did you do?" Lucy's evident pain filled Rebecca with concern.

Lucy cleared her throat and regained her composure. "Well," she said, "At one point my husband was really on fire for the

Lord, and every devotion time we had was so inspiring. He got revelations from the Scripture and grew in the Lord daily. But then he saw the fallacies of the Amish church and questioned and challenged some of the rules and traditions we practice. I have a sister who left the Amish, because her husband read the Bible too much and questioned the traditions of the church. I didn't want to go down that path, so when my husband talked in that direction, I threw a fit. I cried and bawled and told him I was never, ever going to leave the Amish church. I wouldn't listen to anything he said if it in any way questioned the Amish church.

"Finally, he conceded and I won a victory. Or so I thought. But we lost our joy and zeal for God. My husband became nonchalant and lost his enthusiasm and fire for the Lord and the Scriptures. I lost something valuable, and I don't know if I'll ever get it back."

Lucy sighed heavily and turned to put away the stack of plates she had dried. She took a deep breath and let it out slowly. "I still hope we can find the Amish church that is scriptural, and I had hoped that with your husband being a minister, he could maybe help us make this church into that kind of church."

They were interrupted by Rachel who came in saying, "Mom, Dad wants to know if you are ready to go home. He's ready when you are. Please, please tell him you aren't ready," Rachel pleaded. "We aren't done with our game yet."

Rebecca was glad for the interruption, so she could get her thoughts together before answering. Then she was spared answering at all by the men who came in as she rounded everybody up to go home.

New Wine

On the way home, Rebecca held the baby in her lap with one hand and grasped Jonathan's coat tail with her other hand. She didn't want him to tumble off the seat, as they bounced over the ruts in the trail. Her mind replayed her earlier conversation with Lucy.

A sigh escaped her lips, as she thought about how many times they had hoped to correct the problems in the Amish church and always ran up against the same spirit of legalism. *The letter of the law kills.* Trying to fix this centuries-old church by putting new practices in it was like … a thought struggled to form in the back of her mind. Something she'd read. Oh yes, it was in the Bible. Jesus had said something about putting new wine in old wineskins. She would have to look that up when she got home.

After they arrived home and got the children to bed, Rebecca reached for her Bible. "I think I just got a revelation," she said to Lester, as he settled in the recliner. He glanced at her with the question in his eyes. She said, "Where in the Bible does Jesus talk about the new wine in old wineskins?"

Lester reached over and picked up the concordance from the stack of books by his side. After scanning a couple pages, he said, "Matthew 9:17."

Rebecca eagerly flipped the pages and found the verse. "*Nor do they put new wine into old wineskins, or else the wineskins break, the wine is spilled, and the wineskins are ruined. But they put new wine into new wineskins, and both are preserved.*"

She looked up from the page and searched her husband's eyes. "Is that what we are trying to do when we think we can fix the Amish church by making new *Ordnungs*? Do we think our way is the right way?" She asked this more for herself than anyone else.

Her shoulders drooped. "But then I can just hear someone say, 'So quit trying to bring in new ideas and new *Ordnungs*. It'll just ruin the Amish church, and the Amish church must be good to have survived so many years!"

"No, no," she addressed her imaginary but very real adversary. "Look at that last sentence where Jesus said, 'Put new wine in new wineskins, and they'll both be preserved!'

"It doesn't say that anything will be preserved with the old wineskins; it says they'll be ruined. But if we put the new wine in the new skins, it will be preserved. That's like when we say, '*off with the old and on with the new.*' Or that we need to put off the old man Adam with the sin nature and put on the new Adam of redemption."

Rebecca paused and gazed out the window at the bright moonlight shining through the trees. It lit up the back yard so bright she could see deer walking right up to the house.

Lester climbed into bed and patted the mattress beside him. "When you get done preaching to yourself, you could join me."

"Oh, I'll never get done preaching to myself." Rebecca's voice drifted off as she basked in the serenity of the moment.

And Deer

Rebecca stepped closer to the window. The moonlit scene absorbed her, as more deer jumped over the fence and gathered ever closer to the house with the others. For a moment, she forgot her husband was waiting for her in bed.

"Oh, it's just so graceful how those deer can leap over a fence. And now they're so trusting. They come right up to the house to eat grass," she said softly.

She watched a couple more leap elegantly over the fence and join the others grazing; then she quoted Psalm 18:28-29.

For You will light my lamp; The Lord my God will enlighten my darkness. For by You I can run against a troop, By my God I can leap over a wall. She paused thoughtfully. "I love that." She picked up her Bible again and fumbled to find the Psalm. Here it is. She placed her finger on the moonlit page.

As for God, His way is perfect, The word of the Lord
is proven; He is a shield to all who trust in Him.
For who is God, except the Lord? And who is a
rock, except our God? It is God who arms me with
strength, And makes my way perfect. He makes my
feet like the feet of deer. (Psalm 18:30-33)

"My, I love that! Here I was just admiring the agility of the deer, and God's Word tells me I can have *feet like the deer*! And He *sets me on high places*. Oooh, seriously, it really says that? Well, so I guess the Amish aren't that far off when they say we went *hoch* (high). We are going higher. Who'd want to go lower anyway – hell is about the lowest place there is, I think. Of course, I know the Amish mean lower is humbler, but they are deceived."

"Are you coming to bed?" Lester's tired voice called to her from the bed.

"Yes, yes, of course I'm coming, but just give me a minute, this is so good."

He teaches my hands to make war, so that my arms
can bend a bow of bronze. You have also given me
the shield of Your salvation, Your right hand has
held me up, Your gentleness has made me great. You
enlarged my path under me, so my feet did not slip.
(Psalm 18:34-36)

Rebecca closed her Bible, set it down, and sat on the bed. "Now that is such a good word, I believe it will help me through anything life can throw at me." She slipped under the covers and rested her head on the pillow.

CHAPTER 26

Silence the Man

Rebecca rocked the baby in her arms, as she listened to the activities on the other side of the blanket curtain. Church services were being held in the shop today, and the curtain separated this little area from the rest of the shop. Mattresses and blankets on the floor made a good place for the babies and little children to take naps, and the rocking chairs made it possible for mothers to take care of their babies' needs and still listen to the preaching.

She snuggled the baby in her arms and listened to the voices rising and falling in the closing hymn. *I'm grateful for this corner of the shop.*

When the preacher announced that all members were to stay seated at the end of the service, she decided to stay where she was rather than disturb the sleeping child.

She wondered what the purpose of the members' meeting would be. The tension seemed almost tangible that morning, when she shook hands with the women and girls before finding a bench to sit with her little ones by her side. The women were friendly but strained, trying to hide their uneasiness. Rebecca felt sorry for them. *It must be very difficult to be in their positions. Many are kind, loving Christians, just still clinging to the Amish traditions.*

She sighed as she thought of the words of Paul in 1 Corinthians 11:18 where he said, *There are divisions among you.* Yes, the Bible was so true and so simple to understand with the help of the Holy Spirit, but that still didn't make it easy for everybody involved.

Rebecca's thoughts came back to the present when a mother came for her baby and then walked out. She unintentionally left a gap in the curtain for which Rebecca was grateful. It gave her a view of the bench where the ministers sat. Lester sat with head bowed, glancing at the other preacher beside him who nervously clasped and unclasped his hands. A heavy silence fell over the remaining congregation. Finally, after a quick check to see that only members were present, the other preacher rose to his feet and cleared his throat. He shuffled his feet and nervously cleared his throat again.

Lord, help the poor man, Rebecca prayed silently. Her heart went out to this man who was obviously under some great pressure. The preacher clasped and unclasped his hands again, then lifted his head, cleared his throat once more, and said, "I have to tell you . . ." His voice trailed off. He tried again. "I have to tell you . . ." He shuffled his feet and wrung his hands in agony. Tears rolled down his cheeks, and he desperately blurted out, "I can't tell you what I was told to tell you." The bench creaked as he sat down heavily and supported his bowed head in his trembling hands.

A palpable silence reigned over the roomful of people, till a couple of the older women looked at each other, got up, and started preparing the food to feed everybody.

Rebecca slowly released a long breath she had been holding. *What was troubling the preacher so much? What was he supposed to say that he wasn't able to say?*

Later she found out he was supposed to announce that Lester was to be silenced in the ministry. The bishop had sent word that Lester was not allowed to preach anymore.

The Plot Thickens

Sunday rolled around once again, and the other minister had called for another members' meeting after church. Joseph stood with Eli and Marion some distance away from the other boys out by the barn. They all looked up toward the house. They saw Lester and Rebecca come out and stand near the porch. A moment later they were joined by Ora Jay and Irene.

The boys glanced at each other; then they looked at their parents.

"Do you think they will do it today?" Marion asked under his breath.

"I don't know, but I'm ready." Joseph felt a thrill as he realized that two of his best friends were in the same situation as his family was. They might all leave the Amish at the same time.

A few minutes later their parents were called back inside. Marion kicked at a clod of dirt.

Eli muttered, "I hope they do it!" The other two nodded in agreement. Leaving the Amish would be exciting.

That Saturday night as the group of families gathered for prayer, the others asked Ora and Lester, "Well, what happened?"

Ora laughed, "We have too many friends. It didn't work that time!"

The church needed a majority vote to put the *bann* on a member, and they couldn't get enough votes that day so the Grabers and Eashes were still members.

CHAPTER 27

I Will Never Leave You nor Forsake You

Rebecca straightened to stretch her back. She scrutinized the surrounding forest, while she rubbed her lower back, before she bent over to pick more peas. She'd never had peas grow like this. Each state and climate they moved to had taken an adjustment to learn what grew best and how it grew. In all, she'd planted gardens in Tennessee, Arkansas, Wisconsin, Michigan, Missouri, and Texas. *But never peas like this.*

With the cool weather here, the rhubarb grew to an unbelievable size, which made for lots of delicious rhubarb crunches, pies, and jams. The peas grew almost taller than she was, so she could stand and pick a lot of them. And the green beans were amazing. They just kept bearing. She could pick a bucketful of green beans without moving the bucket, and they were such nice beans, not full of insect bites and holes. They had canned over a hundred quarts for themselves and given just as many to others in the church who hadn't been so fortunate.

Sweet corn was a favorite, and when a rancher farther down the valley offered them a plot of land to raise sweet corn, they eagerly accepted because their garden was up against the mountain. They still had snow covering their garden spot when the people down the valley were planting.

The tomatoes and cucumbers needed a greenhouse to get a long enough growing season. Everybody had a greenhouse attached to their garden or close by to raise those things that needed more growing days.

Carrots were an easy crop that did great, as was cabbage. Early in the spring, before the gardens were producing, Ruth gathered watercress along the edges of the lake, which offered a welcome addition to salads and sandwiches. In the winter they grew alfalfa sprouts for greens. Actually, Ruth grew them. She diligently grew the sprouts and spaced them at intervals that provided a continual supply, especially after they bought special lids to drain the jars of seeds properly. Ruth conscientiously learned from people who had lived in the area a while and gathered new ways to eat healthy. Rebecca was grateful for her daughter's industrious ways to help stretch their food supply.

Rebecca's hands busily picked peas, as these thoughts ran through her mind and while she cast regular glances toward the tallest trees surrounding the garden. The reports of bobcats in the area and even lynxes lingered in her mind. Even though a ten-foot solid board fence surrounded the garden, she was sure those wild cats could climb trees and leap right over the fence. *I wish the garden wasn't so far from the house.*

A noise in the trees leading toward the national forest that bordered their rented property checked her thoughts. Her eyes scanned the branches. What a relief when she spied two squirrels jumping from branch to branch. Wildlife hadn't really bothered her till one day when she looked out the kitchen window and saw a mountain lion slinking along a trail at the edge of the forest. Since that time, she wished the garden was closer to the house. Then, when the children wanted to come find her, it wouldn't be so far away.

One day a clumsy old moose charged through there and took a fence out. Entangled in the wire, it dragged the old, dilapidated fencing across the clearing between the house and garden. It caused a terrible ruckus until it finally freed itself and ran off on its way. The fence had been in such poor condition, but still posts and wires had to be replaced.

Once she finished picking the peas, she paused to take in the beauty of the blue, blue sky overhead. Her thoughts turned to the Lord, the Creator of all this awesome beauty. Thinking of the Lord and Jesus brought to mind the incident she'd heard someone relate about an Amish preacher who became convinced that the Amish church wasn't biblical. He struggled and struggled with his convictions, wanting to be sure he didn't make a mistake he'd regret, especially since it involved all his children and the example he'd be to the rest of the Amish people. Finally, one day he knelt in his hay barn and cried out to God. He asked God to just show him Jesus. "If I could just see Jesus, then I'd know I'm doing the right thing," he prayed. Lo and behold, he looked up, and there was Jesus right in front of him. He was overawed in His presence and never had a doubt about leaving the Amish after that. Rebecca sighed as she thought, *That would be nice to have all doubt removed and have a testimony like that.*

"Lord, could that happen to me, too?" She prayed as she reached down to pull a weed from the pea patch.

Blessed are those who have not seen and yet have believed. (John 20:29)

Startled, Rebecca hastily looked around. It was almost as if a voice had spoken those words, but then she realized they came more from inside her, from her spirit. She trembled, weak-kneed and dropped to her knees between the rows of peas. The presence of the Lord was there with her.

I will never leave you nor forsake you. (Hebrews 13:5)

Those words echoed through her mind as she praised the Lord through her tears and thanked Him for hearing her and giving her the answers she needed to build up her faith, to be strong and of good courage, and to follow in the footsteps of Jesus.

CHAPTER 28

Separation from Dad

Rebecca laid the baby in the crib and tucked the blanket around her. She glanced at Jonathan on the couch, absorbed in a book. The clock struck two, as she pulled out her chair and settled down to quilt. She had about an hour before she had to check the yogurt, and hopefully, she could finish this strip and have the quilt ready to roll another round when Ruth came home from school to help her. It was so much easier to do with two people.

Rebecca pushed the tiny needle in and out and pulled the thread through the fabric. Her fingers worked, but her thoughts were in a turmoil. So many things were happening that it was hard to comprehend. Questions whirled through her mind. *Are we doing the right thing? Is it okay to go to those camp meetings the neighbors invited us to attend? Aren't camp meetings worldly? Is it really a good idea to have so many discussions using the English Bible with the families wanting to join the Amish, rather than spending that time teaching them to read it in German? That is the rule of the church – they have to learn to read German if they want to join the church.*

This led her to question herself more personally. *Were we*

wrong to come here where they are so far advanced that they even use bicycles? Should I have agreed to let the children ride bikes to school? And what about the fact that they took on the bike shop to repair and rent out bikes? Her dad's words echoed in her mind. When Rosemary was born, he'd said that this time he saw a row of bikes in front of the house. Then he asked if he'd see a row of cars and trucks there the next time he came? *Will we end up like that?* She wondered.

"Mom." Jonathan brought her back to the present as he asked her to tell him about a picture in the book he was looking at. "What are they doing here?" he asked.

These times at the quilt with the older children in school were usually the times he came for his share of her attention. He had so many questions. If only she had someone who could answer her questions as easily as she could answer his.

The afternoon passed quickly, and as she put the last tiny stitches in the quilt, bikes clattered against the porch, followed by hurried footsteps. The children were home from school.

Rebecca stood to loosen the pins along the back of the quilt and asked Ruth to help her wrap the quilt another couple rounds forward, so it'd be ready to quilt the next day. As she stretched and pinned the quilt, she listened to Rachel's chatter about the new girl at school and how she could now walk home with two friends instead of just one.

All at once, Rebecca made up her mind. She had to sort out all these thoughts in her head or they'd drive her crazy. She made a list for each of the children, so they knew what they had to do before they could play. Then she turned to Ruth and said, "Watch the little ones. I'm going for a walk up the mountain." Jonathan begged to go with her.

"Not this time," she said. "You stay with Ruth now."

She grabbed a coat and scarf and put them on as she walked out the door, across the porch, out the walk, and up the trail that led to the mountain. She sometimes joked that they couldn't see the mountains because of the mountain. Some people had a wonderful view where they could see the mountains against the sky, but here they were right at the foot of the mountains and in the trees.

Rebecca ascended the trail and absorbed the quietness of the forest. The peace penetrated her very soul. When she got to a little clearing at the top, she found a log to sit on. There in the beautiful afternoon sunshine, she poured her heart out to God.

"O Lord," she said. "I don't know if I can do this. Lord, I love my family. I love the Amish lifestyle. I love the German language. I love the community frolics and get-togethers. Lord, I don't want to lose my connection with my nieces, nephews, cousins, and friends. I want my children to know their uncles and aunts and grandparents. Lord, you know how important families are, you know better than I do."

She got up and paced back and forth in the clearing. "Why can't we just serve You and still follow the old ways, Lord? Do we have to change? I don't want to lose my children to the world.

"Oh God," she groaned, fell to her knees, and knelt at the log. Tears rolled down her cheeks. "Oh Lord, heavenly Father, please, please don't make me be separated from my dad. Oh God, I can't do that. I want to be with my dad as he grows old and take care of him as he took care of me when I needed him. I can't do this!" She beat her fists on the log and sobbed. "Lord, I lost my mother when I was little; I lost my baby before I had time to enjoy him; I don't want to lose my dad. I want my children to know their grandpa. This is more than I can bear, Lord. Couldn't You just make the end of the world come right now, Lord? Then I wouldn't have to make all these decisions. Lord, just come get us all now, right now, before we totally mess up.

"And God, this isn't even fair. I know Jesus suffered a lot to save me, but Lord, Jesus always knew He had Your approval.

He always knew You would be there for Him – that You would never leave Him or forsake Him. And now You are asking me to leave my father. That is more than even Jesus had to do, Lord.

"Lord, are you hearing me?" She looked up toward the sky. "I can't do it. I can't have my dad turn his back on me. You said we are to honor our parents. How is it honoring them when we break their hearts by leaving the old ways?"

The words tore from her throat in a scream but sounded muffled in the great silence of the forest around her. Gradually her sobs subsided, and she sat on the log again, blew her nose, and wiped her tears. She felt spent.

As she soaked in the peaceful surroundings, her thoughts went to Matthew 10:37-38.

He who loves father or mother more than Me is not worthy of Me. And he who loves son or daughter more than Me is not worthy of Me. And he who does not take his cross and follow after Me is not worthy of Me.

She lifted her eyes again to the blue, blue skies above the trees. "Yes Lord," she said in a soft voice. "I will follow You. I love You more than anybody on earth, and I want to do Your will. I will take up my cross and follow You, but You sure aren't making it easy."

"God hath not promised,
     Skies always blue;
But God hath promised to be with me,
     All the way through."

She made a song out of the words as she surrendered her will to the Lord. It was time to go back to her family. Her heart was at peace.

As she got to the foot of the mountain, she met Lester coming home from work. He was excited about an invitation he'd received for a meeting. A traveling evangelist and his family were visiting one of the neighbors that very evening. "Can we all eat supper quickly and go?" Rebecca responded to the eager anticipation in her husband's voice and hurried to get supper ready.

As the sun slipped behind the trees and darkness enveloped the mountains, a group of people gathered in the living room of a beautiful log house half way up the mountains on the other side of the lakes. The evangelist had his wife and children sing some songs before he opened his Bible and announced, "Tonight I'll be teaching on the suffering of Christ."

Rebecca sat riveted to his words. What was he saying? Christ didn't suffer in agony because of the physical pain? Well, yes, the physical pain was bad enough, but the real agony of His suffering was because He had to face the disapproval of His Father, because He had to become a curse in his Father's eyes, and because he had to see His Father turn His back on Him and let Him be tortured and die. "Jesus had to take all of our sins upon Himself and become a curse in God's sight, which separated Him from His Father."

Rebecca's heart stood still as remorse flooded her soul. *Forgive me Lord*, her heart cried. *Forgive me for saying I have to suffer more than Jesus did. I didn't realize what He really had to suffer. Oh Lord, it is true as it says in Hebrews 4:15 – For we do not have a High Priest who cannot sympathize with our weaknesses, but was in all points tempted as we are, yet without sin.*

Thank you, Lord, thank you for taking time to answer my questions. Lord, you did it even better than I answer Jonathan's questions. You sent this man and his family clear across the states to come here just to answer my questions. Yes, Lord, I will most certainly take up my cross and follow you. Nobody, not father not mother, not sister or brother will stand between me and You.

I will believe what the Bible says and follow Your teachings. Lord, just show me clearly and I will follow.

CHAPTER 29

Saturday Night Prayer

R uth hugged baby Rosemary and watched their parents walk out the door and down the driveway. The baby twisted and squirmed in her arms, stretched toward the door, and wailed for her mama. To help settle her down, Ruth picked up a book with large, colorful pictures. Usually Rosemary loved it when she sat down to look at books with her. But not tonight. The baby pushed the books aside and sobbed and reached towards the door where she had last seen her mother. Ruth tried to sing to her as she rocked her, but the baby's wails and sobs drowned out her singing. Finally, Ruth just bowed her head and let her own tears mingle with the baby's tears while they rocked. Gradually the baby wore herself out, and the sobs subsided.

Ruth wished she had a book to read but didn't want to risk the consequences, so she wiped her tears and resigned herself to holding her baby sister until her parents came home. She understood that they wanted to go to the prayer meeting by themselves the first time, but she hoped the whole family could go after this.

At least we got to go to the camp meetings, Ruth thought as she rocked back and forth in a soothing rhythm. She loved camp meetings with the fun of canoeing, and she enjoyed listening to the ladies' conversations. The ladies at the camp had so many interesting and often humorous stories to share with each other.

People's testimonies during the camp meetings of how they came to know the Lord captivated her. As they talked about their relationships with the Lord, they made Him seem so real. She'd never heard people talk about Him like that – about having a relationship with God – not just trying to be good and hoping He liked you enough to let you go to heaven when you died.

She wished they didn't have to skip the Sunday morning camp meetings to attend the Amish church, but she understood that it was for the best. After all, her dad could still preach to the congregation. *At least for now.*

As Ruth rocked her baby sister, her thoughts drifted back over the last several years. The move to Montana had turned out to be the best move her family had made yet. *This is a good place to call home.* The days were never boring or monotonous. Things weren't totally pleasant, but they were always interesting. Like earlier in the day, when she had to do something about the lost dust pan. She hadn't been able to find it since Thursday, so she finally told Mother about it. Mother helped search for it. After their fruitless search, Mother said, "The only other place it could have gotten to is in the trash." Ruth jumped on her bike and peddled up to the green boxes where they took their bags of trash. Those green boxes were designed with heavy lids to keep the bears out.

As Ruth struggled to lift the heavy lids on the big containers, she glanced over her shoulder toward the trees at the edge of the forest. *What if a bear comes out while I'm here by myself? And worse – what if a grizzly came?* A couple of grizzlies were spotted a few weeks earlier, but grizzlies were a protected species, so the men didn't dare openly shoot them. The proper thing to do was to report it to the authorities, and they would tranquilize them and take them into the national forest farther away from human habitation. As these thoughts went through Ruth's mind, she reached in and pulled out a couple bags. When she saw some with blue drawstrings tied in a slipknot, she knew they were theirs, as Mother always said not to knot it in case they needed to open it.

The boys at school had talked about how they just needed to do the three S's and get rid of the bears. At first, she didn't know what they meant, but then Dad told her that it meant, "Shoot, shovel, and shut up." That left her thinking. *They'll have to do a lot of shoveling because grizzlies are huge.*

She poked one of the bags and didn't feel anything. When she poked the second bag, she felt the edge of what might be a dustpan. Gingerly, she opened the bag. A putrid odor exploded from the bag. She quickly turned her head and gasped at the smell of rotten eggshells. Holding her breath, she steeled herself as she reached into the squalid mess. Sure enough, her fingers touched the dustpan. Ruth tightened her grip on it and pulled it out. She turned her head to take a deep breath and then held it as she retied the bag and tossed it back into the container. She gulped for another breath of fresh air and dropped the heavy lid. As she biked back to the house with the recovered dustpan, she breathed deeply of the pure mountain air.

Yes, each day brought its own challenges, but since she had accepted Jesus for her Savior, she met them with a joy she hadn't had before.

Footsteps on the porch brought her back to the present. Relief flooded her soul, when she heard the familiar voices of her parents.

CHAPTER 30

Rumors and Gossip

Rebecca stooped to pick up the bobbin that had dropped and rolled under the sewing machine. Snippets and pieces of green material littered the machine, as she sewed new shirts and dresses for school clothes. After retrieving the runaway bobbin, she straightened and picked up the last shirt she'd sewn. There had been just enough material left to make a shirt for Jonathan, even though he didn't go to school yet.

Ruth stood at the kitchen sink, measuring alfalfa seeds and getting another jar started for sprouts. Over by the pantry door, Joseph struggled to open the five-gallon bucket of wheat berries to grind a batch of flour for the weekly bread baking.

The door burst open and Rachel bounded in. "Karen's coming up the driveway." Karen was a single girl and a frequent visitor at the Grabers.

Rebecca smiled a welcome at Karen as she breezed into the kitchen and set a brown paper bag on the table.

"Hi." Karen greeted everybody as she rummaged through her bag. "I was so hungry for some of my favorite peanut butter bars that I decided to come use your kitchen to make them. That way you all can help me eat them because, believe me, I would

eat the whole pan full if left to myself. And I don't need that!"
Karen talked as she reached for the bowl and spoon Rachel
brought her at the mention of the bars, which they all liked.

"Have you heard the latest rumors going around?" Karen
asked. She paused with her measuring to look at Rebecca who
was sorting through the button box to find enough of the same
kind for Jonathan's shirt.

"I don't know." Rebecca shrugged with her focus on the
buttons. Maybe she'd have to put slightly different ones on
the sleeves. It took so many buttons when the shirt buttoned
all the way down.

"Well, down at the store, I heard them talking about you
all, and they said you've been having groups get together to
study the Bible in English. They said you read the Bible too
much. You know there's a moderation in everything." Karen
paused for breath and saw Joseph standing there with his hands
on the doorknob. She demanded, "Aren't you supposed to be
grinding wheat?" Then she turned and noticed Ruth standing
at the kitchen sink listening. "Don't you have something else
you need to be doing now that you're finished there?" Turning
to Rachel, who leaned on the table and hung on every word,
she said, "You've helped me enough, you can go. You all need
to get more done around here to help your mom. She can't be
doing everything!"

With that, everybody disappeared. Soon the steady rotation
of the wheat grinder sounded from the washroom, while Ruth
got a book and retreated to the couch where she wasn't visible
to Karen but could still hear every word.

Karen leaned towards Rebecca and asked, "Doesn't it bother
you about all these things being said about you? Doesn't it just
make you sick?"

"Well no, I can't say it does." Rebecca calmly laid the buttons in a neat row on the sewing machine.

"But they're saying you all went to some camp meetings too, on a Saturday night, just before church. Then Lester preached at the church here the very next morning! I heard some of them say Lester has to be stopped, and they're going to talk to the bishop about it." Karen chuckled as she leaned close to Rebecca and said, "I even asked the one man why he doesn't go talk to Lester himself instead of always running to the bishop. You know what he told me?" She paused, then with a dramatic fling of her hands, she said, "He said there was no way he could talk to Lester about anything like that, because Lester was always so friendly and how can you admonish someone who just stands there smiling at you?

"Oh, I can't even tell you everything that's being said about you," Karen said. "But seriously, doesn't it bother you? Don't you just want to tell some folks what you think about them?"

"No." Rebecca shook her head. "If they want to find something to talk about, they will. I'm not ashamed of any of the things that are true, and in the end, the truth will come out if some are spreading lies. You know, if we're right, we don't have to prove it, we just have to live it." She smiled and quoted,

> Yes, people will talk,
>   The saying is true;
> They will talk about me,
>   They will talk about you.
>
> Though we live like an angel,
>   With circumspect walk,
> Our efforts are useless,
>   For the people will talk.[2]

Karen slid the pan of bars into the oven, which created a lull in the conversation. She walked over to where Rebecca worked and

---

2   *Stove Mounters' & Range Workers' Journal*, "People Will Talk," Vol. 13-14, p. 14.

in a low voice said, "The thing that tops it all off is something I overheard Sunday night after the singing. Two of the boys were talking, and the one asked the other, 'Have you heard what all those Grabers are up to?' And the other one said, 'Nothing would surprise me about them anymore. Why the next thing we know they'll probably be making their own movies!'"

CHAPTER 31

Feed My Sheep

When the bishop came from Ohio to deal with the church problems on the West Kootenai, he arranged a meeting with the ministers. At one point, he looked directly at Lester and said, "We need you to go and talk to Levi about still having rubber tires on his wagon. He needs to change that soon, and you need to go talk to him about it."

Lester hesitated and then said, "No, I can't go. I won't go talk to someone about a simple thing like rubber tires, when he isn't the only one in the church who has them. And besides, that's not what I'm ordained to do. I was ordained to preach the Word."

The bishop blinked once and stared wide-eyed at such open resistance, but Lester hadn't jumped to this conclusion on the spur of the moment.

When Lester was ordained that day in early December at the age of twenty-two, the seriousness of the occasion and calling rested on him. He didn't know a lot about being a minister, but his uncle lived in the same church at the time and guided and mentored him through the basic parts of being a minister in an Amish church, especially for that first year.

There were humorous aspects as well. For example, on one of the first Sundays Lester took part in preaching, during lunch the bishop leaned over and said, "You know, Sundays are to be a day of rest, but we ministers work harder on Sunday than on other days of the week."

As Lester had considered the words used in the charge he'd been given at his ordination, it occurred to him that his charge was "to preach the Word." From that point, Lester always walked in what he felt was true to that charge and tried to focus on the Word of Scripture at all times and not get sidetracked into preaching about the customs, standards, and traditions of the Amish.

In every community and church that he'd been a part of until this last one in Montana, he was never charged with going to erring members to admonish them. He had joined groups sent to talk with someone several times, although he was never the one in charge.

The reality of the gospel of the Lord Jesus Christ pressed itself upon Lester over the years. Instead of always standing over people to watch their every move or misstep and to discipline them for not obeying the standard to the last dot and letter, he saw the importance of preaching the Word and discipling people in faith.

Someone had given him a booklet a few years earlier, and eventually Lester settled down to read it. It was called *Feed My Sheep* by George Warnock. In this book, George built upon the premise that we are all sheep in the pasture of the Master. It pointed out that even leaders and pastors are but sheep, representing the true Leader – Jesus. Many times in years gone by, leaders had grown tired of waiting on the Master; they took the reins of leadership away from Jesus and did what was good in their own eyes. This had continued through generations, as young ministers like Lester, when he was ordained, thought they had a model of tradition to follow in fulfilling the office of minister in the Amish church.

In George Warnock's opinion, what the church leaders of today really needed to do was to become so absorbed in a personal relationship with Jesus that Jesus would become the true leader of the local churches – that we are *all* just servants, or sheep in His pasture. Jesus would build His church, and we needed to step back out of the way and become sheep ourselves, instead of going on in the flesh and building a church the way we wanted it.

This book influenced Lester a lot. More and more, he saw the importance of Amish ministers focusing on the Word, instead of on all the little things they had always focused on – like buttons, snaps, rubber tires, and other things that could easily get them sidetracked and lose their focus on the Word and helping the congregation to grow in Christ. As a congregation grew in Christ, the little things would be taken care of.

So, as Lester adopted this mindset, it changed the way he viewed sheep and shepherds, and it affected the way he led the church in Montana. He wasn't the bishop, but since there was no resident bishop, he was in charge under the leadership of the bishops in Indiana and Ohio who had been given oversight of the district in Montana.

Lester thought back to the Sunday school issue they faced when they first came to Montana; now bigger issues faced the church, and Lester felt like the bishop was singling him out for traditional deacon work – to go talk with wayfaring members. So, when the bishop asked him to visit Levi to ask him to get rid of those tires, Lester was able to respond in truth and say, "I was called to preach the Word and disciple the people in the Word of God. If you want those tires removed, you will have to go and do it yourself."

Besides all that, in Matthew 16:18, Jesus said He would

build His church. Jesus gave us the charge of feeding His sheep – preaching repentance and remission of sins (preaching the gospel and making disciples). *He said to him the third time, "Simon, son of Jonah, do you love Me?" Peter was grieved because He said to him the third time, "Do you love Me?" And he said to Him, "Lord, You know all things; You know that I love You." Jesus said to him, "Feed My sheep"* (John 21:17). *Repentance and remission of sins should be preached in His name to all nations* (Luke 24:47). *And He said to them, "Go into all the world and preach the gospel to every creature"* (Mark 16:15). *Go therefore and make disciples of all the nations, baptizing them in the name of the Father and of the Son and of the Holy Spirit* (Matthew 28:19).

As of This Day

Once the bishop realized Lester wasn't going to be controlled, he changed tactics. He met with Lester again. "I'm going to ask you a question now, but I don't want you to answer it until Sunday in church. Do you still believe in the Dortrecht Confession of Faith, and are you willing to support the *Ordnungs Brief* or not?"

On Sunday the bishop called for a members' meeting. He cut right to the chase. Lester responded to his questions. "Yes, I agree with the Dortrecht Confession, but I don't agree with the way you apply the article on church discipline."

"What about the *Ordnungs Brief*? Do you agree with it?" The bishop's face was impossible to read.

"The *Ordnungs Brief* deals with our styles of clothing and things like hats, what size they should be, how wide the brim should be, and how tall the crown should be, which all depends on whether you are in the ministry or whether you are a lay member. We have issues here that are much deeper than clothing. We have actual spiritual problems that have biblical answers." Rebecca prayed for her husband as he tried to answer without compromising his beliefs but in a way that the bishop would hear what he was saying.

The bishop grew impatient. "Give an example."

"Well, hats for example." Lester tried to stay focused. "The Bible has nothing to say about hats."

"I don't care what the Bible says about hats!" The bishop's flushed face and raised voice were easy to read now. "That's the way we've always done it, and that's the way we're going to continue doing it!"

The bishop couldn't get a unified vote to put them all in the *bann,* but he decided to take things into his own hands and silence them. At the end of that meeting, the bishop told Lester, "As of this day, you can no longer preach in an Amish church." Along with Lester being silenced from preaching, Ora Jay was silenced from sharing a testimony in any service, and Rebecca and Irene were no longer allowed to have a voice in the vote. And none of them was allowed to take communion in the Amish church any longer. That's when Lester and Rebecca decided there was no reason to attend the Amish church services anymore.

Nobody ever came to tell them they were in the *bann* as is the custom when it is officially done. Instead, people just shunned them as they would those under the *bann* of the Amish church. The people at the local store owned by the Amish told them they couldn't sell them anything, because they were no longer allowed to take money from the Grabers as part of the shunning process.

CHAPTER 32

Black Hats in the Driveway

The peaceful, satisfying feeling of a Saturday afternoon pervaded the Graber house. Rebecca sighed contentedly, pulled up a chair, and reached for her needle and thimble. Ruth came to join her, and they stitched away, enjoying the atmosphere of a clean house and food in the pantry in preparation for Sunday dinner.

They had moved the quilt to the far end of the kitchen to make room for the school desks in the living room. The kitchen was a bit crowded, but today it felt cozy with the whole family gathered around and busy with free-time projects.

Lester sat in his chair in the living room reading the Bible.

Ruth gasped. "Mom!" She reached over and touched her mother's arm. "Look." She pointed toward the window. Rebecca lifted her eyes and followed Ruth's gaze.

Ruth rushed to her feet. "Dad," she said in an urgent voice. "Someone's coming."

"Who? Why are you so alarmed?" Lester looked up from the Bible.

"I don't know, but they're coming up the driveway, and they all have black hats. A bunch of them. They must be preachers, maybe bishops." She watched as another and yet another black hat became visible through the trees bordering the driveway.

Lester stood, adjusted his collar, and peered out the window. Sure enough, it was a bunch of them, and he didn't recognize any of them. *Oh, maybe that one's familiar.*

Lester met them at the door, and the spokesman of the group asked if they could come in a bit. Lester held the door as they filed in and stood holding their hats. "Find a seat, find a seat," Lester invited, as he wondered where he was going to sit. In fact, he'd much prefer standing, but then that would be considered odd. He saw his wife and daughter Ruth bringing chairs from the kitchen and hurried to help them. Soon everybody was seated.

Rebecca and Ruth retreated to the kitchen and sat at the quilt again. "Oh Lord, help Lester stay calm and give him wisdom on how to answer anything they come up with," Rebecca prayed under her breath, as she steadied her hand to keep her stitches uniform. She didn't feel called to stay in the living room, because there were no women visitors.

As Rebecca continued quilting, she listened to the conversation in the living room. These were a bunch of ministers and bishops from back East who were concerned about the things they heard about this Graber preacher on the Kootenai. They stopped in to see if they could persuade Lester to stick to the old ways, to the traditions of the church he had been ordained to uphold. They reminded him of the seriousness of the position he was in, having been ordained to be a preacher of the Amish church.

As the voices in the living room droned on and on, Rebecca's mind went back to a couple weeks earlier. They had been going about their daily schedule of school when she looked out the window and saw black hats bobbing up the driveway. But those black hats had been accompanied by some black bonnets, and it turned out to be two of her brothers and their wives and a sister from back East.

When Lester's family had come to visit, they had written and told them when they expected to be there. She would always remember that visit because Rosemary was just a year old and had walked clear across the Koocanusa Bridge on her own two feet. Rebecca held her hand, but Rosemary loved walking. She was so full of energy that Rebecca decided to let her walk.

The Miller twins, Rosemary's cousins, Merle and Verle, were six weeks older, but they weren't walking yet. She smiled to herself, as she remembered how fascinated the three little cousins had been with each other. The twins scooched and crawled after Rosemary wherever she went. Rosemary enjoyed the attention for a while, but when it got overwhelming, she climbed the stairs to the girl's loft and sat at the top, looking down at the twins who couldn't climb the stairs yet. That had been Lester's family.

Rebecca's family came completely unannounced. "As if they were trying to catch us at something," she mused to herself. "Well, I hope they caught us loving Jesus and living our lives accordingly."

Rebecca's heart tightened as she remembered that visit. Her brothers and their wives were restrainedly friendly, eating and visiting and going to church with them till the last day. After breakfast, the men stayed seated at the breakfast table, talking. The hours stretched on and still they talked. The women washed dishes and made lunch, and still they talked. Finally, just as lunch was about to be served, the second brother got up and said, "As far as I'm concerned, Lester and Rebecca are in the *bann,* and I can't eat with them anymore." He got his wife busy packing up to leave. The rest of the party ate together, but then they left.

The silence that fell on the house after they left was broken when Joseph nudged Ruth and said, "Look." He pointed at the floor under the table.

"I saw that too," Ruth said as she saw what her brother was referring to.

Black scuff marks from nervous foot movements covered the floor under the table where their uncles sat. The place at the end where Lester sat wasn't scuffed at all. They would always remember how calm their dad remained in the midst of all the nervous accusations from their uncles.

CHAPTER 33

Denying Christ

Rebecca lifted the cup of cold mountain spring water to her lips, leaned against the kitchen sink, and gazed out the window at the peaceful scene. How grateful she was for this delectable drinking water, so like the water in the dear home they'd chiseled out of the wilderness in Tennessee. For a moment, she let her mind wander to those cherished days in the foothills of the Smoky Mountains in Tennessee.

Those were such wonderful years of working together with her husband and growing a young family. Wistfully she thought of the homestead they'd carved out of those woods and all the hopes and plans they had of raising their family and having that as the old Graber homestead. Tears welled in her eyes when she remembered the turmoil and misunderstandings that led them out of Tennessee.

Why can't people just love and forgive and do as Jesus taught in the Bible? Why does greed and self-righteousness and dissension have to creep in?

Her thoughts returned to the present, and she wiped her eyes, when she spotted Jonathan trudging toward the chicken house with a bucket of water. She smiled as he paused, set the bucket down, and craned his neck. He peered up into a big spruce tree. *He's trying to identify that bird in the branches above his head.* Jonathan wanted to keep up with his older brother Joseph in the number of birds he could see.

Rebecca's thoughts were interrupted by Joseph's voice. "Mom! Mom! Telephone for you." He had been doing the laundry when the phone, which hung on the washhouse wall, rang.

"It's Aunt Mary from Virginia," he said, as she reached for the phone.

"Hello."

"Well, hi there," came Mary's voice from far away Virginia. "How are you doing?"

The love and concern in Mary's voice brought tears to Rebecca's eyes. After the recent visit from her brothers, she didn't know what to expect from her family.

They talked about the weather and the children a bit; then Mary asked, "So what is this that I hear about you denying Christ?"

"Denying Christ?" gasped Rebecca. "What are you talking about?"

"Well, one of the brothers who was out there to visit you wrote in the family letter that you shouldn't be included in the letter anymore because you are leaving the faith and denying Christ."

"How can he say that?" Rebecca tried to swallow to clear the emotional lump that formed in her throat caused by the fact that her brother would actually say that about them.

"But listen to what Dad wrote," Mary went on. "He wrote that when we get to the judgment day we just might be surprised who gets to go to heaven and who doesn't. We shouldn't be so quick to judge each other."

Rebecca closed her eyes and thought, *That sounds so like Dad to say that.*

"So how are you going to keep your children protected and on the right path if you leave the church and its guidelines?" Mary asked kindly. "Do you really believe we shouldn't have any rules to guide us? I mean Jesus often talked about sheep as an example of His people, and even sheep need a fence to keep them in the pasture. The rules of the church are just the friendly fence to keep the sheep from harm."

Rebecca took a deep breath. "But Mary, don't you see the example of the Good Shepherd taking care of the sheep? When the sheep follow the Shepherd, they don't need fences. The sheep hear their Shepherd's voice and follow Him. It's when there is no shepherd that you have to build fences to keep the sheep together."

Rebecca waited as silence hung between them; then Mary said, "The next thing you'll probably tell me is that the Holy Spirit is in the car too, instead of the buggy."

"Oh, but the Holy Spirit can be in the buggy as well as in the car if I'm in it, because when I accepted Jesus for my Savior, I received the Holy Spirit too," Rebecca answered instantly.

"Well, I just wish you all could come join us here, because the church here is so much more understanding of spiritual things, and we really try to live by the Bible," Mary said as she prepared to hang up.

After they ended their conversation, Rebecca sat and thought. She felt nothing but love and concern from her younger sister, while she'd felt such critical judgment from her brothers who had traveled all the way out there to confront them.

The Deacon and the RV

"Mom, Mom, somebody's coming," a chorus of voices reached Rebecca, as she hurried from the bedroom with an armful of clothes to be washed.

"Who is it?" She rushed to the window to see. A modern

RV pulled up the driveway and stopped in front of the house. The children crowded around her as an Amish man climbed from the passenger seat and slowly walked toward the gate.

As he came closer, Rebecca recognized him as someone from a community they lived in a couple years earlier. He was a deacon now. "What's he doing out here in that fancy rig?" she asked herself as she went to the door.

She opened the door but didn't invite him in, because she didn't know his mission. And he was definitely on a mission. He cleared his throat nervously and then tried to ask jovially, "So this is where you all found a place to hide away? Where's Lester?"

"He's at work." Rebecca was about to tell him where he could find her husband, but he interrupted her.

"So, we hear that you are leaving the old ways and are even going so far as getting behind the steering wheel yourself." He took a step forward and tried to peer past her into the house, probably to look for a TV or some electrical appliance that he could report to carry back to his church.

But Rebecca and Lester had been very careful not to violate any church rules about material things. If they were put out of the church, they didn't want it to be said that they were put out because of possessing so-called worldly things such as electrical appliances, cars, and the like. If they were put out of the church, let it be known they were put out for Christ's sake.

Rebecca stepped outside, closing the door behind her to block his view into their privacy. She looked him in the eye and said, "So you would judge us and say we are going to hell if we drive our own cars, but you ride around in a setup like that?" She gestured toward the modern RV parked in the driveway. "I guess you think it's more righteous to pay someone else to sin for you."

The man took a step back as if she'd slapped him in the face.

"Well, we just wanted to stop by to say hello." He cleared his throat nervously as he retreated down the walk and out the gate.

"Next time bring the family," she called after him, but he didn't seem to hear her as he hurried into the RV and directed the driver to drive on.

Joseph stood watching the RV drive out the driveway. "Mom, wasn't that Ivan from back where we used to live?"

"Yes." Rebecca looked at Joseph. "Do you remember him?"

"I think so; didn't you and Dad do chores for them one time when he was sick?"

"Yes," Ruth cut in. "And they made Rivel soup when we were there. I remember that well."

As Rebecca went back to her laundry, she thought about how her children watched everything they did. She hoped they wouldn't be traumatized by all of this happening now.

CHAPTER 34

Lifting the Curse

M om, Mom."
Rebecca sat up with a start to see Rachel's silhouette in the darkened bedroom doorway.

"My nose is so stuffed up I can't breathe," Rachel said. "And Jonathan is crying because his throat hurts."

Rebecca threw off the quilt and shot to her feet. She rummaged through her remedies, until she found the eucalyptus oil, put some on a hanky for Rachel to breathe in, and tucked her back into bed with an extra pillow to elevate her head.

As she went to get a glass of water for Jonathan, she glanced at the clock and saw it was 2:00 a.m. She sat on the side of the bed and rubbed camphorated oil on Jonathan's throat; then she massaged his feet and rubbed his back till he fell asleep.

As she rose to her feet to go back down the stairs, Ruth moaned softly from her bed. "My throat hurts so bad I can hardly swallow," she said. Rebecca brought her some vitamin C and garlic capsules to take with a glass of water, applied the camphorated oil to her throat, and massaged her feet.

When Rebecca walked back to the living room, she opened the wood heater to add more wood. Joseph came down the ladder from his loft, croaking and dragging his comforter and pillow with him. He had already had a sore throat the evening before. She placed her hand on his forehead. *He's burning up with a fever.* Rebecca helped him get settled on the couch, brought him a drink, and then sat down to rub his feet. Before she was done, Lester came stumbling out of the bedroom. "I'm so miserable," he rasped. "My chest hurts so bad I can hardly breathe when I lie down." He started coughing and wheezing. "Then I can't sleep," he gasped between his coughing fits, as he reached for the little bucket by his chair to spit the phlegm in that he'd coughed up.

"Shall I make you some hot tea?" Rebecca wondered as she tucked the comforter under Joseph's feet.

"It hurts too bad to swallow anything." Lester wheezed with each breath and settled in the recliner by the stove.

Rebecca armed herself with the camphorated oil, an old t-shirt, and some hand towels. She draped the t-shirt and towels over the teakettle on the wood heater. They would get good and hot while she rubbed the oil on Lester's chest and back. After thoroughly rubbing the oil into his skin, she laid the hot cloths against his back and chest and brought a blanket to cover him in the chair.

Then she stepped into the bitter cold on the porch to get more wood and picked up the last two pieces with a sigh. Nobody had felt good enough to carry wood last night. The roosters crowed as she walked back inside. She glanced at the clock. *Already 5:30.* As she opened the door of the stove to poke in more wood, Lester stirred on the recliner, then mumbled under his breath, "Guess I'll try the bedroom again." He rose to go to the bedroom but changed his mind and headed for the bathroom. As he turned, the blanket he'd wrapped himself with swirled out and caught the little spit bucket. Rebecca watched in horror, as the bucket went spinning and overturned, depositing the contents on the floor at the end of the couch.

Joseph gasped and pulled his blanket over his head. Lester struggled with another fit of coughing, unaware of the mess left in his wake, and hurried on to the bathroom, while Rebecca grabbed a bunch of old newspapers to sop up the slimy mess, before she got a bucket of hot soapy water to scrub the spot thoroughly. After she dumped the water and washed her hands, she stood by the stove to dry her hands in the warmth, before venturing out in the cold for more wood.

She hurried to the bedroom to get dressed only to find Rosemary whimpering in the crib. Lifting her out of the crib, Rebecca carried her and her blankets to the living room. She made a nest for her to snuggle at Joseph's feet on the couch.

Endless Need for Water

After Rebecca dressed, she hurried to the kitchen and got the fire going in the kitchen range. She took the teakettle to the little pitcher pump to fill it up. The pump just whooshed dry air. She grabbed the water set aside for priming the pump and eagerly worked the handle as she slowly poured water into the pump head. No welcoming gush of water poured out. "Please no, you can't be frozen. I need water," Rebecca pleaded under her breath and frantically pumped, but to no avail. This had happened before when temperatures dropped below zero for too long. The water line froze. *Well, there's nothing we can do about it except wait for the weather to warm up.* She checked the water in the pitcher. *Enough for oatmeal.*

She cooked oatmeal and set it on the back of the stove, while she bundled up in coat, scarves, boots, and gloves. Her breath froze and hung in the air as she paused on the porch steps to decide which task to do first. She headed for the woodshed and heaped an armful of wood on her one arm. She clasped her other arm firmly over the bundle and trudged to the house with the frozen ground scrunching beneath her steps.

After stoking both stoves, she gathered the water buckets and headed for the lake. She flexed her fingers as she jiggled the empty buckets back and forth to keep her blood circulating. The snow crunched under her feet. When she reached the lake, she found the ax – frozen to the ground. She kicked against the ax handle with her booted foot and jarred it loose. She beat her hands against her chest to warm them and felt the blood tingle in her cold fingers. She grasped the frozen handle and chopped at the ice in the lake. Chips flew as she hacked away. Finally, her efforts were rewarded with a slushy sound, followed by a gurgle as she hit water. She willed herself to keep chopping until the hole grew big enough to dip in her bucket.

When she drew out a bucket of water from the icy stream, the drops froze on the outside of the bucket with a crackling sound, as she poured water into the other buckets. She carried two buckets in her right hand and one in her left. Halfway up the driveway, she searched for a level spot to set the buckets down. When she found it, she paused to place the end of her scarf over her mouth and breathed deeply. The cold air hurt her lungs, but the scarf softened the harshness enough, so she could catch her breath. After a moment, she picked up the buckets and resolutely scrunched her way to the house.

Once inside, she set the buckets down and removed her glasses, which had instantly fogged over. Ruth sat on the rocker close to the stove, rocking a whimpering Rosemary who slid to the floor and came pattering across the cold floor as soon as she saw her mother.

"Oh Rosemary, I'm too cold to touch you," Rebecca said as she rubbed her hands together. "Go back and let Ruth hold you, till I get warmed up."

Jonathan had curled up on the couch with Joseph, while

Rachel huddled in the recliner. Rebecca hurried to collect some heavy blankets and sleeping bags to make a bed by the stove. "Rachel, you can lie down here when Dad wants his chair back," she said as she spread out the makeshift bed.

After putting the stainless steel bucket of water on the stove to boil for drinking, she proceeded to make tea and toast for the children. She also brought them oatmeal. Then she made a large cup of hot peppermint tea and went to find her husband in the bedroom. She found him propped up against a stack of pillows, so he could breathe better. He shook his head in protest, motioning that he couldn't swallow. Rebecca took a spoonful of tea and encouraged him to put it in his mouth. "If you quit swallowing completely, it'll just get worse," she warned him as he valiantly tried to swallow the hot tea. After repeated tries, he got about half a cup down.

Rebecca went back to check on the children. Soon she came back with hot lemon juice sweetened with honey. She had no fresh lemons, but she figured the bottled Real Lemon was better than nothing. Lester tried his best to swallow some of it, but he didn't get much down.

"When you come out on your recliner again, I'll rub more camphorated oil on your chest," she told him as she left the bedroom.

Ruth looked so miserable that Rebecca persuaded Rosemary to cuddle on the sleeping bags by the stove with Rachel, so Ruth could go lie down again.

Rebecca bundled up again and went to feed the hens. She broke the ice on their water trough and was relieved to see they had enough for at least another day. She retrieved half a dozen eggs from the hens sitting on the nests and stuffed them in her coat pocket to keep warm till she got to the house. Before returning to the house, she threw a chunk of hay over the fence for Root Beer, the pony, while taking care not to smash the eggs hidden away in her pocket.

Rebecca took the eggs inside and headed for the lake again with the water buckets. They needed water for drinking and washing dishes, flushing the toilet, and if anyone wanted to bathe, it would have to be a bucket bath, till the water started running again. While at the lake, she chopped a hole for the pony to get a drink on his side of the driveway.

When she arrived back at the house, everybody seemed to be dozing, so she headed back out and worked to build a huge pile of wood on the porch to be ready to face another subzero night.

After stirring up the fires, she opened the pantry doors and surveyed the shelves in search of something to cook that the children could stomach. Her eyes lit on a jar of chicken broth. It gave her an idea. She yanked opened the bucket where the homemade noodles were stored, relieved to see it was still half full of noodles. *Thank you, Lord.* She opened the chicken broth, poured it into a saucepan, and set it on the stove. When it started boiling, she dropped in the noodles. As soon as the soup was ready, she brought the children more tea, vitamin C, and garlic capsules to swallow and coaxed everybody to eat some soup. "It'll soothe your throats and give you the strength you need to get better."

"I want a baked potato," Rachel said.

"I thought you're the one who always likes soup!" Rebecca exclaimed.

"Right now, I just want a baked potato," Rachel repeated. "That's the only thing that sounds good."

After Rebecca wrapped a potato in aluminum foil and put it in the oven, she went back to taking care of everybody's needs. When the potato was soft, she split it and added a generous dab of butter. She carried the saltshaker in one hand and the bowl with the buttered potato in the other and approached her daughter.

As Rachel reached eager hands for the hot potato, the light in her eyes repaid her mother for the extra effort it took to prepare it.

All afternoon she had rubbed feet, applied oils, and kept drinks within everybody's reach. She had also opened some of the home-canned grape juice for those who cared for it. Nobody ate much, so there was plenty of leftover soup for supper.

Nighttime and More Sickness

As the long, weary day drew to a close and nighttime settled over the valley, Rebecca felt a sore throat coming on. She thought of what they had learned in the Mark Bubeck meetings about spiritual warfare. She renewed her prayers, not just for her family to be healed, but also for resisting the sickness coming on her. "Don't accept anything that is not from God," Mark had preached.

Well, I'm sure sickness on a mother with a family of sick ones is not from God, Rebecca thought to herself, as she wearily lay on the bed to rest a bit later that night. She didn't bother to undress except her shoes, as she needed to keep the fires burning all night and be ready if someone needed her.

After about an hour, her husband's tossing, turning, and wheezing woke her. His breathing sounded worse than ever. *Should I go for help? Should we go see a doctor? But how can I get him to a doctor?*

Rosemary toddled into the bedroom crying. She wanted to climb in bed with her mother.

"Dad needs room to turn over," Rebecca told her, as she picked her up and put her with Rachel on the bed on the floor. She lay down beside her, got her settled, and patted her back till she fell asleep. Then she got up and went to see if Jonathan was covered.

Her throat burned like fire. *It's getting worse.* She made herself some hot lemonade and forced herself to drink it.

After checking on the fires and making sure everybody was covered, she eased her weary body back into bed. Just as she dozed off, a wail from Rosemary made her jump up so suddenly that she had to grab the side of the doorway to steady herself. Her head spun, as she hurried to see what Rosemary wanted. She didn't want her to walk on the cold floor, even if she'd put warm stockings on her feet.

As she carried Rosemary to the bathroom, she breathed a prayer of thanksgiving for indoor plumbing. Even if she had to carry water to flush the toilet, it was better than outdoor toilets and chamber pots to be emptied. So far none of the drains had frozen. For that she was thankful.

After Rebecca got Rosemary settled, Rachel asked for a drink, and then it was time to stir up the fires again. As she put more wood in the kitchen range, she took inventory of the water supply. She could use the dishwater and bath water for flushing the toilet, but there still wasn't enough to last the day. She glanced out the window. The moon shone so bright on the snow, she could easily see to go for water. She decided to make another water run before it was time to make breakfast. *Before I start feeling worse.* Ruth burned hot with fever now and so did Joseph and Jonathan.

Dealing with the Devil

She bundled up, grabbed the buckets, and headed for the lake. "Thank you, Lord, that we can get water here." Her words formed frosty balloons in the bitter cold air. "What if I had to go all the way to the neighbors?"

As she plodded along, she wondered how long she could

keep going. *If I can't, who would help us?* she asked herself. All of their families lived back East, and even if they lived close by, they wouldn't want to have anything to do with them.

When she stooped over to dip the bucket into the waterhole, she grew so dizzy she had to stop and steady herself. She pressed her gloved hand against her throbbing head as she prayed, *Oh Lord, help me take care of my family. Help me resist the devil. Help me know what to do.*

She took in a deep breath and let it out. Then she said out loud, "Devil, get away from me and my family, in Jesus's name. I will not accept anything from you. I will not allow this sore throat and dizziness to make me sick. In the name of Jesus – leave!"

Her voice sounded muffled behind her scarf in the silence of the snow-laden mountains, but inside it gave her new courage to fight back and not give up. *Jesus is the victor and the devil is defeated.* "Jesus is in me, so I'm walking in victory," she said to herself as she picked up the buckets.

Rebecca trudged up the path with the buckets of water clinking against each other; her thoughts returned once more to her family. If she did ask them for help, would they come? Or would they tell her, "This is what happens because you left the Amish. This is your punishment."

She thought of all her brothers and sisters, her aunts and uncles, and most of all her parents, praying that they would come back to the Amish. How did they pray? What if, instead of prayers of help, they were actually putting a curse on them? She remembered how Mark Bubeck had said people can put curses on each other, but he also explained that you could pray against the curses and break them or send them back to where they came from. *What if so many people are praying for us to come back into the dark realm of religion, that the devil is using that as a curse on us?*

She walked toward the house so fast that she had to gasp for breath when she set one bucket down to open the door. Once inside, she set the buckets by the sink and started peeling off gloves, scarves, and coats and hurried toward the bedroom. She almost ran into Lester, as he was coming out of the bedroom.

"You know what I just thought?" Lester said at the same time Rebecca said, "Do you think it would be possible?"

They both stopped; then Rebecca said, "Go ahead, what did you think?"

"I was just thinking maybe someone put a curse on us?" he said.

Rebecca chimed in with, "That's exactly what I was thinking! What if we're under a curse? We've never been so sick in our lives."

Right there, they bowed their heads and joined hands in prayer. "Heavenly Father, we are Your children, and we know You take care of us and would not send anything bad to us. So, by the power of the blood Jesus shed for us on the cross, we resist the devil and command him to leave and take his sickness with him. We will not accept anything that is not from You, Lord. In the name of Jesus, we break any curse that anybody put on us. We break it and send it where Jesus Christ would send it."

They looked at each other wide-eyed. Peace flooded their hearts, minds, and bodies – a real tangible peace. Something had broken off them. Lester climbed back into bed, and before Rebecca finished tidying the bedroom, he was asleep, breathing normally and softly.

With tears of thankfulness in her eyes, Rebecca walked from the bedroom. In the living room, Jonathan sat up on the sleeping bag bed, reading a story to Rosemary. Rachel had fetched herself a glass of grape juice and sipped it, as she sat on the rocker. Ruth stood in the kitchen, steeping herself a cup of tea, and Joseph sat up on the couch and asked, "Is there any oatmeal left? I'm hungry."

It felt as if a Chinook had blown in. A Chinook filled with health and happiness.

CHAPTER 35

Going the Wrong Direction

*R*ing, rinng, ring . . .

"Mom, Mom, the phone. There's a woman on the phone who wants to talk to you," one of the children hollered from the front of the house.

Rebecca hung the last dress in the closet and rushed to the washhouse to answer the phone.

She held the receiver to her ear. "Hello, this is Rebecca."

"Well, hi there yourself," a woman's voice answered. "What do you mean by this letter? You can't be leaving the Amish!"

Rebecca winced as she held the phone farther from her ear.

"Please tell me this is a joke and you aren't even thinking any such thing," the voice paused, as the woman caught her breath.

"Well, it's not what we would have liked."

"Not what you want?" the woman interrupted. "Of course, it isn't. So, don't do it! Why would you do it anyway? What do you mean by that? You're going in the wrong direction, if you're leaving the Amish, just when we're coming in."

Rebecca waited patiently for a pause. When the woman stopped to catch her breath, she found her opportunity.

"You see, the church here silenced Lester, because they don't like us to . . ."

Rebecca's voice trailed off, as the voice at the other end chimed in again. "I don't see how they could silence Lester; why, they don't have anything against you. You are totally living in the rules, and I want you to be Amish when we join, so we can be friends. You've already helped me so much. You can't leave. I want my children to grow up in the protection of the Amish community. I love the Amish and their ways. I want to join them, and I want you to be there for me . . ."

On and on the woman talked, until finally Rebecca said firmly, "Listen, you say you love the Amish and the Amish ways. Well, did you know that they won't take you into the membership class until you can speak German, and you can't be a member unless you take the class and get baptized. Besides, the Amish never accept divorced couples."

Rebecca tried to talk fast enough to say what she had to say before she got interrupted again. "Teach your children the Bible, and find a good church to attend where they really preach the Bible rather than the traditions of men, as is the case so often in the Amish church."

The voice at the other end grew subdued now. "Well, I knew it might take a while to get into the community, but I want to save my children from the world." She hesitated. "What are some of the things you don't agree on with the Amish? I thought all their rules were biblical."

"I've always wanted to homeschool my children because the Bible tells us we are to teach our children, but the Amish don't allow it. They say we have to send them to the church school.

"And tell me what's biblical about this," Rebecca went on. "When I took the membership class to get baptized, I wanted to be obedient to the church rules. I tried my best to comb every hair the right way and tie my cap strings properly, but when they took a vote to see if the church body thought I was ready to be baptized, you want to know what happened?" Not waiting for an answer, Rebecca said, "The deacon and one of the other ministers came to talk to me and told me that I couldn't be baptized because I was out of line. I had a pin in my cape in the back to pin the cape to the collar, and that was against the rules. When I saw them coming to talk to me, I was so scared. I couldn't imagine what I'd done. And when they told me what the problem was, I was trembling so hard that I could barely pull the offending pin out to show them I was willing to obey the rules. I just hadn't realized it was wrong. And for the life of me, I couldn't figure out why one of the other girls or women hadn't pointed that out to me on one of those other seven Sundays I'd been taking classes. Instead, they made me feel like a convicted criminal when the preachers came to talk to me in such a solemn manner."

When Rebecca paused, the voice at the other end asked meekly, "But that wasn't the preachers where you live now, was it? They're different there, aren't they?"

"You be the judge," Rebecca said. "For example, you know Jacob who lives over in the North Fork Valley?"

"Oh yes, he's one of the finest young Amish men I met out there," the voice said enthusiastically.

"Yes," agreed Rebecca. "He is a godly young man who is a good husband and father and probably practices Christianity more than the average Amish. But you know what? Lester was asked to go tell him he couldn't take part in communion unless he quit cutting his hair the way he does."

"What's wrong with his hair?" asked the voice on the phone. "It looked like a good Amish haircut to me."

"That's just it," Rebecca went on. "Some of the Amish think he cuts it too short. The thing is he could be mean to his wife and kids, but as long as he is dressed right and cuts his hair right, he would be accepted at communion. He could abuse his animals and not pray with his family or quit reading the Bible, but as long as he dresses right and doesn't have any material things that aren't allowed by the church, he'll be considered a member in good standing.

"And you know what they tell a woman if she complains about her husband or even if she asks for help in an abusive situation? They tell the woman that if she was being submissive and godly as the Bible teaches, her husband would be good to her. It's her place to be submissive and take what comes and not complain. They say she's to be a helpmate for her husband."

"But surely not all the settlements are the same," countered the voice on the phone. "Surely there are some better than that where they really believe the Bible."

"Yeah surely," Rebecca remarked dryly. "My dad has been looking for that church all his life, and he'll probably be looking for it till he dies, but he's not going to find it in the Amish or any religion for that matter. I used to think surely we could find or make a settlement that is biblical, but when you're building on the traditions of men your foundation is very shaky."

"Well . . . but . . . I really like the way the Amish help each other work and help each other pay their bills when they need help." Her voice lacked its previous confidence.

"It seems that way," Rebecca said. "But the way it's set up, if you're really struggling and get a doctor bill that is huge to you, but still not thousands of dollars, then they'll tell you it's not big enough to warrant helping. And you'll be required to help pay for and replace things you couldn't afford to begin with when some well-to-do person's house or buildings burn down. You're always asked to pay your share, even if your total possessions aren't as much as the part that was destroyed for them.

"Of course, there are Amish people who really live by the Bible, who are kind and loving and help others the way Jesus taught, but they are often not the ones in charge or ordained to be bishops and deacons." Rebecca paused to let her words sink in.

"Well, I'm not ready to give up on the Amish yet," the woman admitted. "I really think you are making a mistake for leaving." Her voice sounded defensive now. "You are going in the wrong direction, I'm telling you!"

"We aren't exactly leaving," Rebecca told her. "We are being put out because we pray without the prayer book, and we teach and preach the Bible in the language people can understand. The Amish can't stay Amish if they tolerate such goings on as English Bible studies and praying in English without the book.

"I really need to go now," Rebecca said. "I'm sorry to disappoint you by not staying Amish. You could save yourself a lot of grief if you didn't try to join them, but I can't tell you what to do."

"Okay, well, don't quit writing. I still want to hear from you." The voice sounded tearful. "Oh, and when you get your next phone statement, let me know how much I owe you. Thank you for taking my collect call." Click, the caller hung up.

"Collect call? What!" Rebecca looked at the receiver in dismay.

CHAPTER 36

Honor Your Parents

One day after another phone call in which one of her cousins who'd been out of the Amish for a number of years shared with her the struggles and doubts he was battling, the Lord impressed upon Rebecca's heart to write to her cousin to explain further:

Dear Cousin,

Thank you for the phone call. It's always good to hear from friendly relatives, but I couldn't get you and some of the things you told me off my mind. I keep hearing you say:

"I regret every day that I left my parents."

"I don't think I will have total peace until I go back to the Amish."

"My parents never mistreated me, so I really had no excuse to leave."

"The church we attended was never unreasonable and on my case."

"The rules were sensible for that lifestyle, and I could easily submit myself to them."

"But I'm married and have children, so I can't leave them

and go back, and my marriage partner wouldn't agree to go with me."

"I feel that every day I don't go back to the Amish I'm disobeying my parents; therefore, I'm living in sin."

Now let's address some of these issues:

> Ephesians 6:1 says, *Children, obey your parents in the Lord, for this is right.*

In the Lord is the key point here. If you go back and join the Amish church, you would not be *in the Lord.*

If you were a member of the Amish church, you would have to practice the *bann* or shun people who are clearly born-again Christians. And that is not being obedient to the Lord.

If you've been born again and accepted Jesus for your Savior, then you are a child of God, and other born-again Christians are your brothers and sisters in the Lord. So, if you don't accept them in love, you are sinning. But you can't accept them and be in good standing with the Amish church.

Jesus said if we love father or mother or brother or sister more than Him, we are not worthy of Him. *He who loves father or mother more than Me is not worthy of Me. And he who loves son or daughter more than Me is not worthy of Me. And he who does not take his cross and follow after Me is not worthy of Me* (Matthew 10:37-38).

It is wrong to require people to dress a certain way and live a certain way, if it isn't required in the Bible, or to tell them they will go to hell, if they don't obey all those rules. The Amish put a person out of the church if they don't obey the church rules. They put them in the *bann.*

In 1 Corinthians 5, Paul wrote about sexual immorality and how we shouldn't eat or drink with such a person who calls himself a brother. Cutting your hair differently or dressing differently or driving a car is not immoral. God looks at the heart, not the outward man.

Our greatest concern should be to make sure we are pleasing God. Being obedient to God and His commandments is showing that we love Him. So, we need to check ourselves. Are we obeying God's commandments? The words we speak every day – are they spoken in love? Do we let words of corruption into our conversation?

Are we free of habits that would dishonor our body, which is a temple of God? Our body is not our own. It was bought with a price, so we should take care of it to the best of our knowledge.

God will give us the strength to get rid of any bad habits. All we have to do is ask for His help, and He will freely give it. Sometimes we need an accountability partner – someone who will pray for us, encourage us, and challenge us to stay on the right track. If we humble ourselves before the Lord, He will raise us up.

He gives grace to the humble. Grace can be defined in so many ways. One example of grace is that it gives you the strength to do what needs to be done to live a holy life.

Being obedient to your parents and honoring your parents are not the same thing. All of us need to honor our parents. If you treat your parents with respect and show kindness to them whenever the opportunity arises, you honor them.

I know some children who stayed in their parents' church and are supposedly members of good standing in the Amish church who don't honor their parents.

If you have asked God to forgive your sins, asked Jesus into your heart as your Savior, and given your life to God, then you are a child of God, and you don't have to feel guilty or afraid of anything. If you fall back into sin in any way, all you have to do is truly repent and God will forgive you again.

Be concerned about your relationship with God first and foremost and your relationship with your parents will be all right in the eyes of the Lord.

Read Matthew 6:33 every day until you believe it. *But seek first the kingdom of God and His righteousness, and all these things shall be added to you.* When you really believe it in your heart, you will live it, and every other problem will be taken care of and never bother you. You will be at peace. Not the peace the world gives but the peace that passes all understanding; the peace of Jesus.

It doesn't say, "Seek your parents' approval." It says, *Seek the kingdom of God and His righteousness.*

God bless you as you seek His will.

Your Cousin,
Rebecca

P.S. You mentioned the Dortrecht Confession of Faith. That was written back in the day by Christians seeking the kingdom of God, and the Confession is biblical. Although the Amish say they still believe those, they don't practice all the truths in them, and they put more weight on their man-made rules and traditions than on the Word and direct commandments of Jesus.

In closing, I must add that it never ceases to amaze me when someone says they feel guilty about disobeying their parents by choosing a different church, but it doesn't seem to bother them to use the Lord's name in vain or to use other curse words in their conversations, or to indulge in habits that are clearly not godly.

They will stand before the Lord God on the great judgment day and will have to answer to Him – not their parents.

CHAPTER 37

Lester Buys a Suburban

Rebecca pulled the curtain across their bedroom doorway, crossed the room, and sank to her knees at the bed. She buried her face in her hands, took a deep breath, and began, "Oh Lord, You know what's going on because You know the end from the beginning. Heavenly Father, You know that Lester is going to bring home a Suburban tonight. Oh God, somehow this seems like a clincher, a statement, and a public declaration of a step across that line of no return. I know they've already silenced us in the church, and my brother has said he has put us into the *bann* and all that, but I guess I could sort of live in denial of it being so final till now. And You know, Lord, when I leave this house and get into that Suburban, I'll be leaving a part of my life behind that I always cherished and held dear – the old-fashioned way of transportation – the horse and buggy days. Lots of Amish people freely get drivers for anything and everything, but You know I wasn't like that, Lord. I was like my dad. I'd rather drive long distances with horse and buggy than get a driver. If I was going to preach and teach that we should drive horses, I was going to practice it too. Oh God, You know this is not easy for me!

"But Lord, besides leaving the old-fashioned ways and all that, there's another reason why I struggle with this. Lord, You know what a battle I've had with carsickness. From as far back as I can remember, I've gotten sick when I rode in a car – and not just a little. Lord, You are my witness that I've had to throw up so many times while riding in a car even for short distances. And God, that is miserable. To think that every time I go somewhere, I'll have to be fighting this carsickness and nausea.

"Can You imagine how miserable that will be, Lord?" she cried. "Every time I go somewhere I'll be trying not to throw up?

"Of course, You know all about it, Lord, because You know everything. But Lord, here's another thought: You made me, so I believe You can heal me." Rebecca struggled with the thoughts crowding to be uttered. *Would it be a sin to try to make a deal with the Lord? Well, maybe it could just be a request rather than a deal. All right, here goes.*

"And Lord, I believe You can heal me of this carsickness. So, if it's not a sin for us to own our own vehicle and drive it, Lord, please take this carsickness away from me and never let me be bothered by it again. Oh Lord, I leave it in Your hands now. I will go with a smile on my face and trust that You are my Helper, and that You are leading us in this next step."

"Mom, Mom! Mom, where are you? Come quick, Dad's coming with our Suburban! He's coming up the driveway right now!"

CHAPTER 38

First Vacation

Lester hummed under his breath as he packed sleeping bags and tents into the Suburban. He loved traveling – always had. He had taken a train ride from Indiana to Missouri when he was six years old, long train rides across the states and into Canada when his mother was doctoring for cancer, and the multiple cross-country bus trips – first as a young man and then later with Rebecca and the children. At times they'd even hired drivers to go on long trips. He enjoyed all of those trips. He loved the feeling of the miles passing and new horizons opening up in front of him, but he was more excited about this trip to Yellowstone National Park than any of those other trips. This vacation was different.

For the first time in his life, he could plan when and where and how he wanted to go without having to contact a driver with a vehicle to arrange an itinerary that worked for the driver and the other people on the same trip. If he decided to take a different route halfway through the trip, stay an extra day, or go to a different place, he could do so on the spur of the moment.

This is truly freedom. It was his vehicle and his family and his trip. God had been so good to them. Energy and good spirits surged within him, as he strode toward the house to see how things were coming along. Rebecca and the girls were in the kitchen getting the food and drinks packed. They were going to be camping and cooking their food over a campfire. They didn't want to forget anything they might need.

Lester came to the door. "Last call! Everybody out!" He glanced back toward the Suburban. Jonathan already sat in his spot waiting. Joseph rummaged through his stuff in the schoolroom. Rebecca picked up baby Dorcas and the diaper bag and headed for the car. Ruth stashed one of the food containers in the car and returned to the house for her travel bag. Rachel and Rosemary settled in their places, Ruth walked back to the Suburban. Lester asked, "Where is Joseph?" Then he heard his son's feet on the ladder, coming down from the loft.

Halfway down the ladder Joseph clutched a box of art supplies and a sketchpad. "I'm coming!" He rushed past Lester and out the door.

Lester closed and locked the door; then he walked toward the car. There was a place for everybody, and everybody was in place. Lester pulled the keys from his pocket and took his place – the driver's seat.

Lester and Rebecca smiled at each other, as they reached to join hands. Lester prayed for a safe trip and thanked the Lord for His provision.

He turned the key in the ignition and they were off.

Golden Days

As they crossed the West Kootenai Bridge, Rebecca sighed with contentment and reached for her bag of sewing. She soaked up the peacefulness of the atmosphere in the Suburban. Jonathan sat between his parents on the front bench seat and pretended to drive. He kept his eye on Lester and copied his moves. Lester checked the gas gauge and talked about how far they would drive that night. How nice to be able to have family discussions as they drove with no concern about the driver listening in. Joseph began a sketch of his view from the backseat. Jonathan held his pretend driving position so well that Joseph thought he would have time to sketch him. It was a beautiful day in June, and they, the Graber family, were going to Yellowstone National Park.

When Rebecca finished sewing the buttons and holes on the little girls' dresses, she folded them neatly and reached for the book she'd been wanting to read but never had time for.

As she settled back in the seat, she breathed a prayer of thanksgiving. *Thank you Lord for healing me of carsickness. Thank you that I can sew and read and write while we drive and never get that sick feeling at all.*

Lord, You are so good to us. I love You so much. Thank you, thank you, thank you Lord!

After a while, Rebecca closed the book and gazed out the window.

"Finished already?" Lester asked.

Rebecca shook her head. "No, I didn't finish it. My mind just kept going in so many different directions that I couldn't think about what I was reading."

"Wow, those must be some powerful thoughts to distract you from reading." Lester knew how involved she usually was when she got into a good book.

"Our life is more interesting than a book these days." She settled back with a contented sigh. "Just think what all has happened in the last two years. It would make a book if it was all written down."

"Why don't you write a book?" Lester asked.

"I'm too close to it yet. Give me another twenty years. Laura Ingalls was sixty when she wrote her famous classics, so I still have time. I'm so busy living right now, I don't have time to write."

Epilogue

My name is Dorcas, and I am the youngest of the Graber family. I am the only one of us who was never Amish. I missed it by just a year. I almost missed even being in this book, but I managed to squeeze in the very last chapter.

When I was growing up, I didn't realize it was unusual that my family used to be Amish. Didn't we all have to put on old, stuffy, long sleeved, ankle length dresses to visit our grandparents who lived in a house that was always hot in the summer, because there was no air conditioning or cold upstairs in the winter? Wasn't it normal to know how to speak a second language and know what liverwurst is? (Trust me, you really don't want to know.)

The older I got the more I realized I was the unusual one and that my Amish heritage was going to be something people would always ask about. So I wanted to have answers and know the actual old Amish ways. Thus began a long game of what I like to call *"So Mom, do the Amish really (fill in the blank)?"* I would ask her and my older brothers and sisters who remembered all kinds of crazy questions, in order to have as much knowledge as possible to answer people's questions. And trust me, there were questions. My whole life has been filled with questions about the Amish as soon as people find out my family used to be Amish:

"Oh, your family is Amish?"

"Are you sad you never got to be Amish" "Do you wish your family was still Amish?"

"Do you still drive everywhere with horse and buggy?" "Was it fun growing up Amish?"

"You're Amish? That's so cool! I thought your clothes looked Amish!"

I usually smile and try to find a polite way to respond without letting out the sarcastic answer trapped in my brain. Like:

"No, we're in a movie theater."

"I super lucked out! Are you kidding?" "No. Like no, not at all."

"I'm literally standing next to our Suburban."

"I was never Amish! That was the rest of my family!" "I wouldn't know since I was never Amish."

"I am not Amish! I'm wearing a short skirt and Converse shoes (a brand of shoes not allowed in the conservative Amish groups)! This is not Amish! Plus my ears are pierced!"

Okay, so yeah, sometimes I find it hard to keep those things inside. But I have gotten better at it.

To be perfectly honest, at first the more I learned, the more I was puzzled. Why were people so interested in the Amish when they lived with such restrictions and fear and no music? (I mean, seriously?) And besides, they had kicked our family out for loving God and doing the right thing! How could there be anything good about these terrible people? People told me about how peaceful the Amish were and how nice the children played with each other, but all I knew was the stories of how they had instilled my mother with crippling fear, and that my cousins I played with were no different from any other small children. We fought and cried and pushed just as much as "English" children.

By the time I was thirteen, I had decided the Amish must be evil and totally didn't want anything to do with them. But then my mom began to tell me stories of when she was little and stories about Grandpa. Those were marvelous tales. Enough to fill a book or a hundred! One day she'll write those books, and when she does, you need to read them.. Seriously. She had the best childhood adventures, and I know from personal experience how amazing my grandpa was.

So maybe there was some good to the Amish? I heard people say that all the time:

"Oh well, at least your family got what was good from the Amish."

Did we? And if so what was it?

Could something be both terrifying and beautiful? The Amish were still the people who kept my mom away from her dad, but my grandpa was also Amish. Opposite sides of the same coin.

Learning your heritage is important, even if it's not what you would like. Sure, I don't have any cool stories of my ancestors being missionaries or soldiers fighting for freedom, but I do have distant cousins who run a cheese factory in France, which is sort of cool.

And please, always feel free to ask me about the Amish.

– Dorcas Graber

Meet the Author

R ebecca Borntrager Graber was born into an Amish family of ten children. She lost her mother at the tender age of ten and later taught school in the Amish parochial schools. She married Lester Graber, who was ordained as an Amish minister the second year they were married. Rebecca and Lester were shunned by the Amish church thirteen years later, after taking a bold stand against some extra-biblical Amish rules.

Rebecca always enjoyed writing and was a frequently published author in *Family Life*, *Young Companion*, and *Blackboard Bulletin*, which were monthly magazines published by the Amish. She has conducted many women's Bible study groups in her home, taught Bible classes at a local jail, and carried on correspondence with prisoners from a variety of jails and prisons.

At present Rebecca, her husband, Lester, and their youngest daughter, Dorcas, live in Fort Worth, Texas, where they are members of Eagle Mountain International Church.

Connect with Rebecca on Facebook

www.facebook.com/mamawgraber

BREAKING THE SILENCE:
THE AMISH AND THE REFORMATION

Available on DVD and Digital. Run time: 54:30

The year 2017 is the five hundred year anniversary of Martin Luther nailing the 95 Theses to the church door in Wittenberg and starting the Reformation in Germany. This film considers the impact of the Reformation Era on the Amish Church in America today.

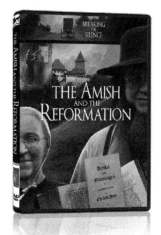

Was the work of the Reformers effective?

This DVD is part of *Breaking the Silence,* a documentary series that presents a respectfully honest view of the origins and legacy of the Amish and how they became who they are today. Featuring the story of Lester and Rebecca Graber's salvation, excommunication, and exit from the Amish church, this film traces the Graber family and the Amish Church back to the Reformation Era.

www.MyAmishStory.com

"A true and honest picture of the history of the Anabaptists, the Amish of today and their religious beliefs. This film could be the beginning of yet another needed reformation – not only within Anabaptist circles, but in church denominations all over the world. People from all walks of life will be impacted and forever changed after watching The Amish and the Reformation."
-Joe Keim, Mission to Amish People

Photos

Log house we built in Nunnelly, Tennessee, in 1986.

Side view of the log house in Tennessee.

Photo of the log house in later years.

Moose were frequently seen on the West Kootenai.

Koocanusa Bridge linking Eureka and the West Kootenai and crossing Lake Koocanusa (the one Rosemary walked across on her first birthday).

Amish schoolhouse on the West Kootenai.

Amish schoolhouse on the West Kootenai.

Graber home on the West Kootenai.

View of house from the bike shop.

Graber home during the winter of 1994.

A photo of the house in 2016.

The Graber's bike shop.

Joseph inside the bike shop.

The row of bikes mentioned by Rebecca's dad.

Larch made the best firewood but we usually found mostly Douglas Fir & Lodgepole Pine.

Winter's Supply of Wood 1993

Each autumn in Montana, Dad would get a fire wood permit. We would go up in the mountains. Dad would cut down dead trees. When the logs were cut in pieces we'd load them on a trailer and haul them home. After splitting, the wood was stacked in the wood shed and on the back porch. Quite often we would do the stacking assembly line, making it so much more enjoyable. Ten cord of wood was usually enough for a Montana winter.

The woodshed and side porch of the house,
stacked with a winter's supply of wood.

Mama's Deer

1993

Joseph's Deer

Deer meat was a vital part of our diet.

Views of our garden on the West Kootenai.

Views of our garden and inside the greenhouse.

Overview of the garden and greenhouse with the bluebird nest.
We left the ladder stationary till the eggs hatched.

Root Beer, the pony – our only means of transportation
besides bikes, before the Suburban.

Quilting was a vital part of our livelihood.

Rachel, Rosemary, and Jonathan perched on a woodpile.

Ruth on Root Beer, the pony, holding Rosemary, with Jonathan
(wearing a hard hat) and Rachel (all in Amish clothes).

Ruth and Joseph in their Amish clothes in the
kitchen at our West Kootenai Home.

Rebecca is holding Rosemary while sitting at the kitchen table.
Ruth is standing beside the woodburning kitchen range.
Jonathan is standing at the table.

Rachel with Jonathan in the background, dressed in Amish clothes,
in the living room of the West Kootenai home.

The Amish buggy and the Graber's first Suburban share the parking space in front of the Graber home on the West Kootenai in 1994.

Lester Graber at the wheel in 1994.

The Graber family in Moulton, Texas, in the late 90s.

Graber family photo in Moulton, Texas, in the early 2000s.

Lester and Rebecca at the film shoot of the *Breaking the Silence* documentary in Indiana in 2014.

Lester and Rebecca in true Amish garb at the film shoot
of *Breaking the Silence* in 2014.

Similar Titles by

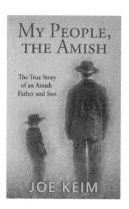

My People, The Amish

Joe Keim paints a detailed picture of life behind the bonnets and buggies. More than a biography, this is an honest look at the heart-warming traditions that mingle with the deep-rooted legalism of the Amish community in Ashland, Ohio.

Born, raised, and baptized in an Old Order Amish church, from childhood Joe Keim was taught that if he didn't follow the twenty-two-page ordinance letter that governed his community, there was no way he could get to heaven. What started as a path of rebellion led Joe and his wife Esther to a caring group of Englisher Christians who would love them like family and show them how to live out their new found faith in Jesus Christ.

Nine months after their traditional Amish wedding, Joe and Esther left family and friends forever to live openly for Christ, and endured shunning and excommunication with bold faith. Since then, the Lord has brought many former Amish people to Joe and Esther for help. Because of their passion for the Amish people and with the support of fellow believers, they have brought biblical truth to thousands of Amish through the ministry they founded in 2000, Mission to Amish People (MAP).

Available where books are sold.

An Amish Boy and a Mother's Prayer

An Amish Boy and a Mother's Prayer takes readers into the heart of Daviess County, Indiana, where Glen Graber was raised Amish. His family was swiftly kicked out of the Old Order Amish church when Glen's dad bought a rubber-tired tractor. Then Glen's mother died, and left him with a request: She had been praying for a business that would alleviate the family's financial hardship, and asked Glen to take responsibility for the family's future. Despite the pressure, Glen and his family found hope and humor as they saw their mother's prayers being answered.

More than a biography, this book is about a boy being determined to change his place in the world, and the miraculous reversals of misfortune. It's about the prayers of a mother, the idiosyncrasies and love of a father, and the strength of a family. It is, in other words, the story of us.

Available where books are sold.

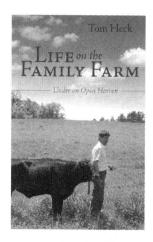

Life on the Family Farm

"You are the most God-gifted writer I've ever had," Tom's college professor told him. However, Tom quit college; his love of farming drew him back to the farm. Thirty years later, Tom picked up the pen again, drawing readers into farming adventures with him. In these exciting and uplifting true stories, he shares his love of farming, family, and God. His unique writing style brings the reader right alongside him and his family as they work on their northern Wisconsin dairy farm.

Tom's stories have spread like wildfire from his hometown newspaper to papers across America. Readers tell him, "Please don't quit writing." Others ask him, "When are you going to make it a book?" Due to popular demand here it is.

From quotes like "Dad, I really enjoyed fixing that with you" to "She's a dead cow don't call me anymore," these engaging stories will keep you turning the pages to read one story, then another. As you do, you will be blessed as so many others have been.

Available where books are sold.

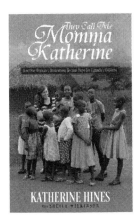

They Call Me Momma Katherine

Do you ever sell yourself short? That's what Katherine Hines did before she realized she was selling God short. After years of tragedies, Katherine learned that God could do more in her life than she ever imagined if she trusted Him and believed. She discovered that He wants to change lives through us and bless us in the process. Whoever we are, wherever we came from, God can use us to make a difference in someone's life.

Katherine's story begins with tragedies, but God touched her heart at a crusade and led her to Uganda as a missionary to the children. Leaving her prestigious job and home, she went to a land of mud huts and polluted water. In the midst of sickness and poverty, she loved and cared for the orphans of the war-torn country, as she faced witch doctors and Muslim agitators. Katherine shares her life story to help us know that we can all make a difference – if only we let God.

Available where books are sold.

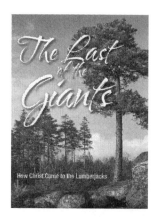

How Christ Came to the Lumberjacks

The Last of the Giants

In its early years, Duluth was a gold mine for lumber barons. Men were employed as lumberjacks and worked like beasts, only to be tossed aside like used equipment when no longer needed. The grand forests were raped for their prime timber, the balance burned wastefully. The men were coarse and hard, but they had to be to survive. More than any other people that ever lived in our land, these old-time lumberjacks could truthfully say, "No man cared for my soul."

That is, until God sent three men to the great Northwoods of our country – Frank Higgins, John Sornberger, and Al Channer. These men blazed new trails of the Spirit and founded an empire for God. They reached a sector of humanity for which no spiritual work had ever been done before, storming the Northwoods with a consuming passion for Christ. And with that passion, they also brought a heart as big as all outdoors, a love for men that burned like a flame, and a desperate desire to see these men saved.

Available where books are sold.

Made in the USA
Middletown, DE
03 January 2021

30699800R00119